JUS
POLITICS

JUST POLITICS

ANDY REED,
GARY STREETER
AND STEVE WEBB

WITH KRISH KANDIAH

Authentic

16 15 14 13 12 11 10   7 6 5 4 3 2 1

First published 2010 by Authentic Media Limited
Milton Keynes
www.authenticmedia.co.uk

British Library Cataloguing in Publication Data

A catalogue record for this book is available
from the British Library

ISBN 978-1-84227-720-1

Cover design by Moose77
Printed and bound in Great Britain by Cox and Wyman, Reading

CONTENTS

SECTION 1:
JUST POLITICS AND
BECOMING INFORMED

SECTION 2:
JUST POLITICS AND DEMONSTRATING INTEGRITY

SECTION 3:
JUST POLITICS AND
FINDING INSPIRATION

SECTION 4:
JUST POLITICS AND GETTING INVOLVED

A MESSAGE FROM THE LABOUR PARTY LEADER
GORDON BROWN

I have always believed that the public square is more than a marketplace. Our common realm is not and cannot be stripped of values – can never be merely a place for calculation, contract and exchange. So I do not subscribe to the view that religion should somehow be tolerated but not encouraged in public life – that you can ask people to leave their faith at the door when they enter a Town Hall or the Commons' chamber.

The Christian contribution to British politics, and to the Labour Party in particular, is immense. For more than 50 years the Christian Socialist Movement has been a prophetic voice to both the Party and the church. Congregations and the Christian charities have been Britain's conscience on issues from debt cancellation to child poverty to the good stewardship of the Earth. Each of these great campaigns mounted by the churches is rooted in the idea that we are each our brother's or sister's keeper. It is that ideal which inspired the Labour Government as we trebled aid and cancelled debt, lifted half a million children out of poverty and signed the world's first ever Climate Change Act.

The financial crisis was perhaps the toughest test yet of our progressive resolve. During the most tumultuous days of the recession, I kept returning to something I first learned in my father's church as a child. In this most modern of crises I was drawn to the most ancient of truths; wherever there is hardship, wherever there is suffering, people of good conscience cannot pass by on the other side.

The lessons of the gospels need not be kept separate from political life. If Christians engage with politics, we can together build a society where wealth helps more than the wealthy, good fortune serves more than the fortunate and riches enrich not just some of us but all. That is why I entered politics, and the vision which inspires me still.

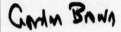

Prime Minister

A MESSAGE FROM THE CONSERVATIVE PARTY LEADER
DAVID CAMERON

It has been a difficult time to be involved in politics. Too many politicians have let the public down, and we have struggled to show why we deserve your support. It makes asking for votes a harder task, but it also reminds me that politicians cannot do it all. Too often we have pretended that we have all the answers and all we need is your vote. I think we are learning that we need to work harder to deserve support, and we need a lot more than your votes.

A stronger society cannot just be magicked into being, or forced through a government programme. It comes first through empowering and enabling individuals, families and communities to take control of their own lives, and second by recognizing that we all have shared responsibility for our neighbours, our country and our planet. Governments have an important role to play, but so do we all.

Churches have a proud history of involvement in schools, hospices and other community organizations. And today, as I travel around the country, I am constantly amazed by the breadth and depth of the church's engagement in society. In communities where government has failed to make much impact it is local groups, often churches, who daily see lives transformed. It is often church groups who lead the way in fostering a culture of mutuality and responsibility – helping each other through difficult times; restoring bonds of trust and respect; effecting change because, although the problems are severe, they know that they are part of the solution.

The wonder of democracy is that we all get to play a part. It is not just about voting, because a responsible society may begin at the ballot box but it continues throughout the years and across the country. It's about offering a helping hand where no one else noticed; motivating communities to love one another; never walking by, but taking time to cross to the other side.

I hope this book will help all believers to engage fully in the political process. Together we can change things.

> The vote is the most powerful instrument ever devised by man for breaking down injustice and destroying the terrible walls which imprison men because they are different from other men.
> US President Lyndon Johnson[33]

A MESSAGE FROM THE LIBERAL DEMOCRATS PARTY LEADER
NICK CLEGG

In my first speech to the Liberal Democrat conference as party leader, I told a story I had heard recently about a little girl doing a painting in class. The teacher came over to ask what she was painting, to which the girl replied, 'God.' So the teacher said, 'But no one knows what God looks like.' The girl said, 'They will in a minute!'

I was talking about the future of Britain – a country full of potential, where hopeful children believe that anything is possible, but also a country where hundreds of thousands of children live in poverty, or fall behind at school.

Unless governments today tackle issues like education reform and climate change, the future will be bleak – especially for our children, and younger people.

As a party, we believe that people should have their say in the key decisions that affect them and their future. It is vital that our younger people participate in elections, which is the most powerful way that the individual can have their say and make the political system listen. The more power and influence we have, the more we will work to give power back to people so that they can shape local services, contribute to their local communities, and write their own future.

I believe that it is vital in this period of uncertainty that those who believe in traditional British values of freedom and tolerance take part in the political process.

Liberal Democrats seek to make our country and our world a better place – and we need to work together to make it happen.

Nick Clegg

The world is too dangerous to live in – not because of people who do evil, but because of people who sit and let it happen. Albert Einstein[41]

INTRODUCTION: A JOURNEY TO POLITICS AND JUSTICE

I thought they were the bad guys. The press never had anything positive to say about them. They just lurched from one scandal to the next, exposing incompetence and conspiracy. They were Big Brother looking down on you, they were certainly not to be trusted, and they were waiting to pounce the moment you put a foot wrong.

That was my view of social workers – until I became one, being approved as a foster carer. When my wife and I began our journey into fostering, any suspicion and standoffishness we may have felt was exchanged for a welcome and a warm handshake as we invited the assessing social worker into our home. Soon they were no longer the bad guys to be avoided, but partners with us as we tried to find ways to work together with them in helping young children and their families get the best help possible. They were not just sinister cogs in the machinery of the care system – they were colleagues motivated by a common passion to serve the needy struggling to make heart-breaking decisions and working with precious little resources.

I have been on a similar journey with politicians. With the spin, sleaze and scandal and the cultural suspiciousness of authority figures, politicians have had a bad press. They have been presented as the bad guys, self-seeking, careerist and hypocritical. With politics and faith being two of the biggest taboo subjects around, I felt that, as an evangelist, I could at least steer clear of one of them. I focused on equipping Christians to pray for their friends, to answer the intellectual objections to faith, to train up preachers and teachers, and to resource the church in creative ways to present the gospel. But as I taught the gospel, I began to realize that the centre of Jesus' teaching was the kingdom of God. For many Christians this was the very reason that politics was irrelevant. They could surround themselves with Christian values, rules and ideals and avoid earthly politics. But Jesus prayed for God's kingdom not to protect Christians but to come on earth. He challenged his followers not to hide from the world but to engage with it – to be salt and light in rotten and dark places. As I began to grasp the significance of this, I realized that privatized religion and soul-saving was not enough.

Karl Marx said that religion was the opiate of the masses; that religion de-motivated people from bothering to change their world because they were just hoping for another one. Religion was a form of escapism, like the drug-induced hallucinations that numbed the pain of reality. I began to wonder if Marx visited our church services whether he would think differently. If he looked around at us closing our eyes in worship, singing songs that focus on our emotions, listening to sermons that rarely engaged with the realities of poverty, injustice and violence, I decided he would nod and say, 'Told you so.' And yet Jesus' teaching brought good news to the poor, freedom for the oppressed, reproofs to the religious elite, and challenges to the hypocrisy of the system. True, Jesus did not wield power to usurp the structures or stand for election but nobody could say he was not deeply involved in the political wrangling around him. And it was not long before he was standing in front of Pontius Pilate on charges of bringing a new political system that was challenging the power of Rome.

Am I my brother's keeper? Genesis 4:9

Just as all this was beginning to dawn on me, I attended a seminar on church in the inner city. After the speaker outlined the social needs of his own area – high unemployment, teenage pregnancy and drug use, he then explained how the only things his church was running were Bible studies and preaching classes. As I listened to him assert that because the church was the only institution caring for the souls of those around, our biggest responsibility was to run evangelistic programmes and leave the social, practical and physical needs to the social workers and politicians, I saw red. Jesus did not always preach and never heal, or provide soul food but never bread, wine and fish. The dualism that prioritizes the soul over the body is closer to Buddhism or Gnosticism than Christianity – the resurrection itself speaks that body and soul go together. When Jesus tells us to love the Lord our God with our heart, soul and mind he is calling us to worship with complete integrity. When he tells us to love God and love our neighbour – regardless of who our neighbour is – he is calling us to show concern for God's concerns and spiritual and practical care for people made in God's image.

When we realize that Jesus' teaching pushes us to get involved in the messiness of the communities and countries we live in, it is tempting to take on the role of moral policemen of the world, focusing solely on issues such as homosexuality, abortion, euthanasia, bioethics and freedom of religion. These are important issues for Christians to be clear on, but if they are the only issues we are known to engage in, we have a double dilemma. First of all, we have to question whether Jesus' priorities are our priorities. The politics of the Bible is far more passionate about championing issues of justice, human rights, and peacemaking, than on campaigning over legislation on hot-button issues. Secondly we should check whether our reputation reflects Jesus' reputation. Jesus' politics labelled him a 'friend of sinners', while all too often Christians involved in politics are labelled 'homophobic, judgemental and insensitive'.[1]

I came from a position that avoided, even shunned, politics, and I certainly didn't want to get into a position that ended up avoiding or shunning the people I was still passionate about evangelizing. I discovered another route one day as I was in Starbucks, looking around me at people, choosing their Fair Trade coffee, with their shopping beside them in their environmentally friendly tote bags. With issues of global justice and environment becoming more mainstream, we have a lot to learn from those Christians that have set the pace in these causes. It was Christians that championed the Fair Trade movement, the cancellation of the debts of the poorest nations, and the anti people-trafficking campaigns.

But it is not only on these large scale movements that we can have a major impact on our communities. As we seek to bless others through our neighbourliness, our work, our community involvement or our vote, modelling our lives on Christ's self-sacrificial lifestyle, we can change society. Even Labour MP Roy Hattersley once noticed this and said, 'We atheists have to accept that most believers are better human beings ... it is impossible to doubt that faith and charity go hand in hand ...'[2]

Pursuing justice and compassion, whether locally, nationally or internationally is the clear call of the Christian. But I still had one more obstacle to overcome. While I was prepared to get involved in politics, I was not quite so prepared to get involved with politicians. That is, until I met some. Just like my prejudice against social workers had been put into perspective when I began working with them, meeting Christian politicians from across the parties who were passionate about their vocation and their faith, changed me. Here were people who, despite the smear campaigns and intense scrutiny into their expenses and personal lives, were seeking to practice what they preached and were honest and upfront about the challenges, opportunities and struggles.

I hope you enjoy getting to know some politicians as you read this book. Some of these politicians are high profile, others live around the corner from me. Some of them do politics for a job, others as a lifestyle. All of them believe that politics, faith and justice can go hand in hand, and they have contributed to this book on the understanding that all proceeds will go towards the work of Tearfund. I hope these politicians will inspire you to become more informed, involved and influential, whether in your Neighbourhood Watch scheme or by standing in the next election, by using your voice, your vocation or your vote.

Krish Kandiah
November 2009

All Christians are involved in politics – they just need to realize it and develop their engagement to be more effective otherwise secularism will simply continue to reduce political freedoms and civil liberties – and therein limit the gospel. Dave Landrum

As one who has with his own hands sorted through the remains of thousands of slaughtered Tutsi corpses, as one who has heard with his own ears the screams of boys being beaten like dogs by South African police, as one who has looked with his own eyes into the dull, blank stares of Asian girls abused in subhuman ways, I hope in the Word of God. For in the Scriptures and in the life of Jesus Christ, I have come to know God – my Maker, the Creator of heaven and earth, the sovereign Lord of the nations. It is through his Word that God reveals his character and it is in God's character, and God's character alone, that gives me hope to seek justice amid the brutality I witness.

Gary Haughen[44]

Section 1:

JUST
POLITICS
AND
BECOMING
INFORMED

THREE POLITICIANS
TELL THEIR STORY

STEVE WEBB

I was brought up in Birmingham where I lived with my parents who instilled in both me and my brother a strong sense of fairness and justice, but it was at university I met committed Christians for the first time. I found they were people like myself who wanted to get things done but who were motivated by the Christian message. For the first time I was presented with a choice about faith, and the verse that eventually clinched it for me was Jesus' words, 'He who is not with me is against me' (Luke 11:23). I realized I couldn't just sit on the fence, so I made a decision to become a Christian. The strands then came together as my academic research was in poverty and equality, my political interests were in the same sphere, and I felt called as a Christian to speak up for the marginalized and the dispossessed.

I entered the political world through joining the London-based Institute for Fiscal Studies, a non-partisan think tank. While offering independent commentary on political issues such as budgets, benefits and manifestos, I met politicians from all the parties who impressed me – Christians and otherwise. I eventually joined the Lib Dems as they held principles and values I respected, they weren't in it for what they could get out of it, and they hadn't joined the party because it was a fast track to power – because it certainly wasn't!

I also met my wife Helen during this period. She was then a curate at my local church in Clapham. We got married and moved to the Bristol area where Helen took up a post as a hospital chaplain. I found myself living in a part of the country that was sympathetic to the Lib Dems, but where the Conservative incumbent had a safe seat which he had won with a majority of over eleven thousand votes in the previous election. It was therefore something of a 'leap of faith' in 1995 to seek selection by the local Lib Dems in Northavon to be their candidate for the 1997 General Election. I knew it would mean giving up my job at the non-partisan IFS; I did not know how I would support my family for the next two years – my wife was expecting our first child – and I had no sense that I was even the front runner. Looking back, getting a job as Professor of Social Policy at Bath University fitted so well it could almost have been planned (!), but at the time it was a huge risk that kept me awake at night.

In May 1997, the General Election arrived and the votes were counted. Everyone expected the Conservatives to win and the local media didn't even bother turning up. But, to almost everyone's astonishment, I was duly elected to serve the Northavon constituency with a majority of 2,137 votes!

I believe that the well-informed, well-educated and well-resourced have plenty of ears to speak to and plenty of doors open to them. Although I represent all 80,000 people in my constituency, I feel a special call to show a bias for the poor whose interests are not going to be represented any other way, and therefore to speak up for the socially marginalized.

GARY STREETER

I was born in 1955 and was raised on a dairy farm in East Devon with my parents and five brothers. I still live in Devon, in the heart of my constituency, in an old farmhouse with my wife Jan, plus a deaf mongrel, a wire-haired miniature dachshund and several horses.

Jan and I married in 1978. She was a Christian and I was not, but within twelve months I, too, became a Christian and we relocated from London to Plymouth. I was working as a lawyer at the time, specializing in company and employment law, and became involved in a busy charismatic house church. Every time I read the Bible the words 'law and justice' kept leaping out at me, and I felt a sense of calling on my life, but I didn't know what that calling was, which was very frustrating. In December of 1985, I went away for a day of prayer and fasting. I was 30 years old, I had two children, I had been made a partner in a big law firm and I was heavily involved in the church, so you can just imagine the reaction when I went home that night and told my wife that God was calling me into politics!

The following Tuesday, over the phone, I joined the Social Democrat Party where David Owen was the local MP. Six months later I was elected – after three recounts – onto the local (Plymouth) council. I knew nothing about politics, and apart from Mrs Thatcher, I couldn't even name one cabinet minister. Like most charismatic Christians in those days I was a 'cabbage for Jesus'. It was 1986, and I was beginning to learn about politics for the first time in my life.

As I did so, I came to realize that I didn't agree with my party on the issues of grammar schools or Europe. I believed in family and individual responsibility. I believed in defence. I loved my country and my Queen – in short, I was a natural Conservative, so I switched parties.

On 14 February 1992, I was on the Conservative Party approved list when Alan Clarke, MP for Plymouth Sutton, announced at the Valentine's Ball that he was ready for the election. But within a few days I got a call from our party chairman to let me know that Alan Clarke had subsequently decided to stand down. On 10 March I was selected from 300 candidates – with no experience of campaigning – and on 11 March, John Major called the election. Four weeks later, I was the MP.

I had a surge of faith a week before the election. I was standing on a doorstep in a struggling neighbourhood after weeks of good and bad conversations, and I looked out over the whole constituency and felt that God was telling me that I could win. But despite hearing God's voice, I was still a bag of nerves on Election Day. As the votes stacked up to an astounding 12,000 majority, it was incredibly moving.

I was very clear that I had entered politics because of my faith, and am still very open that Christianity is the overriding factor in my day-to-day political and family life as I seek to make a difference in the community and in the country.

ANDY REED

It is said that the Labour Party owes more to Methodism than it does to Marxism, and this was very true in my case. I was brought up in the Methodist Church in my home town of Birstall in Leicestershire, who 'politicized' me throughout my teenage years, combining teaching about the Faith with instilling a sense of justice and a sense of community. I developed a strong belief that the message of the Bible was very much based on social justice. However, at the time the idea of actually becoming a politician was foreign – I had this image of Oxbridge graduates who travelled around in chauffeur-driven limousines, and that just didn't happen to people who came from schools like mine.

At that point, I was planning to volunteer to become a coffee-picker in Nicaragua to do my bit to fight off the evil empire of Ronald Reagan's America. I was driven by the stark sense of global poverty and the terrible statistics of children dying around the world from preventable diseases, statistics which remain at a staggering 30,000 infant deaths a day, mainly related to starvation, sanitation, poor hygiene and polluted water. As a teenager in the 1980s the news was also full of our wine lakes, beef and butter mountains. It seemed to me that God had given us more than enough to go round, and that basically politics was responsible for distributing food and water and shelter to the entire planet. For me, giving my life to Christ meant trying to respond to that in the way that I lived my life.

I wanted to change the world, but I was frustrated with the inactivity in the church and I got more involved in political activism. The Labour Party seemed a natural choice for my socialist democratic values, although at the time it felt a bit like a rat joining a sinking ship, as Labour had just lost the 1983 General Election. This fact helped me to quickly rise through the ranks, and I was elected as a parish councillor aged just 21.

Prior to 1992, the Labour Party needed a candidate in Loughborough and I was chair of the local party, so I decided to have a go, mainly just for the experience. Stephen Dorrell was the

> Our political system may have its problems and contradictions, but we need to thank God and acknowledge the historical sacrifice of our forerunners that we enjoy representative democracy that embodies biblical principles such as liberty, justice and accountability. More than most people around the world, we have an opportunity to participate in processes that influence our lives and the lives of those around us.
>
> Andy Reed[32]

Conservative MP with a 17,000 majority so I never expected (or even had ambitions) to become an MP myself, and was busy planning my wedding for later that same year, and a subsequent sabbatical. I expected to lose, but I didn't mind, because I thought I would be able to proudly tell my grandchildren that I had run for office in the same election in which Neil Kinnock was elected Prime Minister! I reduced the Conservative majority significantly that year, and in the following election was encouraged to stand again, especially as local boundary changes gave Labour a fighting chance, and indicated to me that God was opening a door in my own locality, where I felt a real sense of calling.

My calling and journey led to a comfortable win and I felt this enabled me to live out my passion to be a voice for the voiceless, and release the fire in my belly to make a difference in international development. That fire is still burning and keeps me going through the tough times. I still don't wake up every morning thinking I am a politician. I just see myself as a pretty ordinary bloke from Loughborough who happens to be an MP so that I can get things done locally, nationally and internationally.

WHAT IS POLITICS?

ALAN STOREY

Sometimes politics is seen in terms of who gets to power, but that answer is not as simple as it seems. Often leaders seem powerless, and in democracies we want firm constraints and rules about power. What power consists of is deeply problematic. Christian understanding gives us some deep perspectives on politics that actually run under the razzamatazz of the coming election.

First, the focus must not be on politicians, but on all of us. Politics is about a law-abiding society. Jesus made the point graphically in the Sermon on the Mount. God asks all of us to love and abide in law and justice. We are to hunger and thirst for righteousness.

Second, office-holding is about service. Jesus insisted on it. The one who wants to rule or lead must be a servant. Rulers must be humble and focused on what is good for us. Many rulers from Nero to Ceausescu got this wrong. If rule is self-service, it has lost its way and the people sooner or later realize. It seems strange to say that politics is ruler humility, but proud rulers finish up in 'cuckoo land', useless and locked in their egos.

Third, politics is the rule of law over government and governed. Law is often equated with legalism, or rules, but in biblical terms it is far deeper than that. It is loving and respecting all people, even our enemies. As Paul said, 'love is the fulfilment of the law' (Rom. 13:10). It means practising peace, giving workers rest, fair trading, restoring the poor, supporting the weak and providing health care like the Good Samaritan. The law is merciful; it allows new starts. No one is outside the law – not the Prime Minister, the police, the armed forces or BAE systems. When Old Testament rulers ignored the law, prophets held them to account.

Fourth, politics is about the common good. Often we are encouraged to look to our own self-interests, but that way leads to splits, social conflict, racialism and group hostilities. It is because businesses have been greedy that unions have been hostile. It is because bankers have been selfish that they have made a financial mess. Conversely when others are as important as ourselves then families, communities, nations and the planet hang together. We are always about changing empires into common wealth.

Fifth, politics upholds institutions to act rightly. Judges and courts are to be fair, and families places of love and nurture for children. Marriage is to be faithful and tender. Education is one of the primary concerns of Jesus, the greatest Teacher of all. Work is to be fair, good, shared and resourced. Taxation is to be geared so that there shall be no poor among us. Everyone's freedom is to be respected, and those of every faith and no faith can live by their consciences. These are not easy tasks, but every society has to address them.

Sixth, politics must be about truth. Jesus insisted that truth was the basis of his power before Pilate, and told the truth, even when it guaranteed his death. Without truth trust, respect, justice and love cannot flourish.

Seventh, politics is about peace – peace within families, on estates, in cities and among nations. 'They will beat their swords into ploughshares and . . . Nation will not take up sword against nation, nor will they train for war anymore (Isa. 2:4).

'Ah,' you say. 'You have described good politics, not politics as we know it.' 'No,' I say. 'You will find these principles providing the structure for much of our politics.' We are in part law-abiding, have (usually) civil servants, recognize the rule of law, the common good, institutions, truthfulness and peace. But we also mess up in all of these areas. Yet, we best understand the mess – wars, waste and the selfish rich – by seeing these gentle terms of the rule of God. When we see Jesus' good politics, we realize that politics any other way is not such a good idea.

> **He has showed you, O man, what is good. And what does the LORD require of you? To act justly and to love mercy and to walk humbly with your God.**
> Micah 6:8

I know, I have seen, the desperation and disorder of the powerless: how it twists the lives of children on the streets of Jakarta or Nairobi in much the same way as it does the lives of children on Chicago's South Side, how narrow the path is for them between humiliation and untrammeled fury, how easily they slip into violence and despair. I know that the response of the powerful to this disorder is inadequate to the task. I know that the hardening of lines, the embrace of fundamentalism and tribe, dooms us all.

Barack Obama[29]

ORDINARY RADICALS STORY: PATSY

In 1999, Patsy's youngest son Dorrie went out with a friend to play basketball and never came home. They had driven into a cul-de-sac when a group of young men, faces covered, came towards them from the subway on bicycles. Dorrie and his friend knew that this could only mean trouble, so they got out of the car and ran. One of the cyclists pulled out a gun and shots were fired. Dorrie was hit in the arm and then twice in the chest.

Dorrie's was one of several gang shootings that fortnight in Manchester, and one of three fatalities. It was a tragedy that forced Patsy not only to turn to her church community for support, but to the wider community where mothers across the city were mourning because of similar acts of violence.

Some time later, Patsy sat down with a group of mothers who were meeting to discuss what they could do to stem the tide of gun crime and protect their children. Patsy and two others formed a group called Mothers Against Violence and began to discuss what initiatives they could take. They started by talking to fearful and grieving people in the community, to the gang members and to the police.

At first this resulted in local awareness campaigns and multi-agency meetings, and a march in which hundreds of local residents turned out to protest against the war on their doorsteps. As the news of their impact in the community reached the ears of their local MP, their efforts began to take on national significance. Prime Minister Tony Blair met them in 2002 to talk about their concerns, and Patsy felt that finally they were able to influence policies, such as bringing in a five-year sentence for carrying a gun, and be part of other anti-gun government campaigns. In 2004, Patsy received the Woman of the Year award for her dedication to bring peace to the toughest communities, and to offer alternatives to the gangland life of guns and drugs.

Patsy has lost a son and continues to feel pain from that loss, but she has forgiven the killers and describes her campaign work with Mothers Against Violence as a sense of giving birth – giving life back to a dying community.

We are encouraging young people to know that God has given them the nations as their inheritance and has also given them to the world as agents of change. They are conduits of his presence and power in their communities. Patsy McKie

Injustice anywhere is a threat to justice everywhere. We are caught in an inescapable network of mutuality, tied in a single garment of destiny. Whatever affects one directly, affects all indirectly.
Martin Luther King, Jr[34]

CASE STUDY: BOAZ TRUST[3]

We crouched with our knees pressed against our chests unable to move. Each evening we were given a sandwich, a bottle of water and told to keep quiet. Over the next four weeks the boat would stop at different ports and people would be taken from the container.

Eventually, after four weeks, I was the last one left in the crate. The container was opened by one of the first white men I had ever seen! Physically I was totally devastated, I could barely move and I was afraid of everyone. I had never seen so many white people or cars!

The police came and calmed me down. I spent two days in the police station but I didn't know what was happening. I refused food because I was frightened. They took me to the Home Office who asked me how I had come here, and about the reasons why I had to leave and the torture I had been through.

They sent me to Rochdale where I shared a house with other asylum seekers. The people who were working in the hostel were kind to me, they took me to the doctors and the hospital.

When I had an appointment at the asylum court I didn't understand asylum law. I had seen my solicitor only once and he was not able to come to the hearing. The hearing was over three hours long. Three weeks later I had a letter saying I was refused asylum and that I could go back to

Khartoum because it was safe there. This was unbelievable to me. The Sudanese authorities had my fingerprints so I knew as soon as I arrived I would be killed.

One day some people came to my house and said the Home Office have said your file is closed and now you are out. I told them how I was very sick, they could see my condition and it was cold and raining outside. They said sorry, but this is the resolution of the Home Office. Lifting me from my bed, they carried me outside, and sat me on the street with my bag of medication.

I crawled to Rochdale Town Hall. I slept there outside for a week on a piece of cardboard, living on water and bread I had bought from Lidl with my last few pounds. Nobody talked to me. I was under some cover so people from the town hall did not see me. The cover kept the rain off me.

How could you go about befriending Hamed and helping him?

What would it take to give him hope for the future?

You can read the rest of Hamed's story on the Boaz Trust website, www.boaztrust.org.uk, and discover practical ways to get involved in helping the destitute asylum seekers in your communities.

Sittings in the House of Commons begin with two and a half minutes of Christian prayer, which has been common practice since 1567 and is not televised. The speaker's chaplain usually reads a prayer such as the Lord's Prayer, or one of the following, while the members face the wall.

Lord, the God of righteousness and truth, grant to our Queen and her government, to Members of Parliament and all in positions of responsibility, the guidance of your Spirit. May they never lead the nation wrongly through love of power, desire to please, or unworthy ideals but laying aside all private interests and prejudices keep in mind their responsibility to seek to improve the condition of all mankind; so may your kingdom come and your name be hallowed. Amen.[22]

Almighty God, by whom alone Kings reign, and Princes decree justice; and from whom alone cometh all counsel, wisdom, and understanding; we thine unworthy servants, here gathered together in thy Name, do most humbly beseech thee to send down thy Heavenly Wisdom from above, to direct and guide us in all our consultations; and grant that, we having thy fear always before our eyes, and laying aside all private interests, prejudices, and partial affections, the result of all our counsels may be to the glory of thy blessed Name, the maintenance of true Religion and Justice, the safety, honour, and happiness of the Queen, the publick wealth, peace and tranquillity of the Realm, and the uniting and knitting together of the hearts of all persons and estates within the same, in true Christian Love and Charity one towards another, through Jesus Christ our Lord and Saviour. Amen.[23]

IDIOT'S GUIDE TO . . .
PARTY POLITICS

DANNY WEBSTER

When we go to the dentist for a filling, or travel to work on the train, or even turn on the tap, politics is happening. The decisions that are made by elected officials have an impact on every aspect of the lives we lead, so when the chance comes to choose who represents our community in the House of Commons, this is our opportunity to have a say in how Britain as a nation is run. Political parties play a crucial role in our democracy because they put forward alternative ideas of how the country should operate.

In voting for an MP, we are entrusting them to make decisions for the whole of the UK. While they do have a local constituency which they serve and people they represent, their focus is also on national policies. The personalities of candidates, and their views on local issues, will undoubtedly play a role as we decide our vote, but it is through the political party they belong to that we have the ability to influence what sort of government we would like. The laws and policies originate in parliament at Westminster, and politicians should think primarily about the impact on the country rather than on their own patch.

Right now, the biggest issue in politics is the state of the economy, and in the election campaign, each party will be looking to demonstrate that they are the one best able to get Britain back on its feet. A difficult balancing act for MPs is trying to weigh what is in the best interests of the country against what is best for their local residents. Say for example that a car manufacturer, whose future was not financially viable, was, however, a major employer in the constituency. To support a subsidy for the manufacturer might be good for the constituency but bad for the country as a whole. Alongside these questions, there are broader issues at stake. The past two decades have seen huge levels of economic growth, but this has now been shown to have come at a cost. Much of the country's prosperity has been achieved on the back of a dependence on credit. And even the public services that we are now accustomed to are buckling under the imminent spending cuts.

When we vote in a General Election, this is the sort of dilemma that needs to be considered. MPs are often elected with less than 50 per cent of the vote, but when they stand to speak or go through the lobbies to vote they represent every one of their constituents. So before we place our folded slip of paper into the ballot box, we need to think about what is best for the good of the nation, what issues require the attention of our politicians, and check out what each party says in its manifesto.

Politicians, especially when they are seeking our vote, will try to promise us the earth. But we must remember to ask ourselves, as well as the candidates, what the impact of those promises could be. Will efforts to get people back to work come at the cost of those who most need the state's support? Will a return to economic growth be consistent with caring for the world around us?

Once every few years we get the chance to overthrow the government. If we think they've done a decent job of running the country, we can grant them an extension. But when we elect politicians to represent us and make decisions on our behalf, they – as individuals and as parties – always remain accountable to the voters.

DEFINITIONS[4]

POLITICS:
the practice or study of the art and science of forming, directing, and administrating states and other political units

HOUSE OF COMMONS:
the lower chamber of parliament

DEMOCRACY:
government by the people or their elected representatives; a political or social unit governed ultimately by all its members; the practice or spirit of social equality; a social condition of classlessness and equality; the common people, especially as a political force

MP:
abbreviation of Member of Parliament – a member of the House of Commons

CONSTITUENCY:
a district or body of voters who elect one representative to a legislature, or all the residents represented by one deputy

GOVERNMENT:
the system or form by which a community etc. is ruled

WESTMINSTER:
the Houses of Parliament at Westminster in London

PARLIAMENT:
the highest legislative authority in Britain, consisting of the House of Commons, which exercises effective power, the House of Lords, and the Sovereign

ELECTION:

the selection by vote of a person or persons from among candidates for a position, especially a political office

GENERAL ELECTION:

an election in which representatives are chosen in all constituencies of a state

LOBBIES:

groups of persons who attempt to influence legislators on behalf of a particular interest

BALLOT BOX:

a box into which ballot papers are dropped after voting

MANIFESTO:

a public declaration of intent, policy, aims etc., as issued by a political party, government, or movement

REPRESENT:

to act as or be the authorized delegate or agent for

POLICIES:

plans of action adopted or pursued by a government, party etc.

FACTFILE: TOP TEN UK POLITICAL PARTIES ACCORDING TO REPRESENTATION

1 **LABOUR PARTY** (the centre-left democratic socialist party that stands for social justice, strong community and values, reward for hard work, decency and rights matched by responsibilities).

2 **CONSERVATIVE PARTY** (the centre-right party that stands for advancing opportunity, nurturing responsibility, and protecting security).

3 **LIBERAL DEMOCRATS** (the centre party that stands for building and safeguarding a fair, free and open society, balancing the values of liberty, equality and community).

4 **DEMOCRATIC UNIONIST PARTY** (the right-wing unionist party for Northern Ireland that stands for strong leadership in challenging times).

5 **SCOTTISH NATIONAL PARTY** (a left-leaning nationalist party that stands for Scottish independence).

6 **SINN FEIN** (a left-wing Irish republican party that stands for independence from the UK and reunification of Ireland).

7 **PLAID CYMRU** (the regional party of Wales that stands for global justice, local community building and independence).

8 **SOCIAL DEMOCRATIC AND LABOUR PARTY** (a nationalist party of Northern Ireland that stands for reconciliation, unity, justice and prosperity in Ireland).

9 **GREEN PARTY** (a democratic party that stands for social and environmental justice).

10 **RESPECT PARTY** (the left-wing coalition party that stands for peace, justice and equality).

ARMS

I had a dream that was simple enough
I had a dream of a world that had love
Where three meals a day was the norm for every man
Now subsidised lies keep this status quo
Cos anything's better than letting you know
'National Security' covers this part of the plan

When the arms that you use, the arms that you use
Are the ones that are holding the children you lose
When the arms that you use, the arms that you use
Are the ones that are held out, all battered and bruised
You don't understand what's been killing you,
And I'm wishing it wasn't true.

Now we'll give you food, we're the generous ones
But only if you buy our rockets and guns
A bullet tastes better than bread, or so they say
And only nice dictators are buying from us
They're very good customers, don't make a fuss
Business like that doesn't come by everyday.

For the swords will be turned into ploughshares one day
And the nations they will not train for war anymore
They will not, they will not be afraid.

Now you're telling me what I don't want to hear
There's landmines and debt lying wrapped up in fear
Secretly squeezing the life out of this land
So take me away from these facts that I've heard
The back of my head is the place they deserve
Take me away so my conscience remains undisturbed.

Andy Flannagan[46]

Adapted version by
Andy Flannagan of
his song 'Arms', ©
Daybreak Music Ltd.
Admin by Memralife.
Used by permission.

SPEAKER'S CORNER: MILLENNIUM DEVELOPMENT GOALS

REVD JOEL EDWARDS

At the dawn of the millennium, something of a political miracle happened. For the first time a meeting of world leaders took place in New York for what was described as an 'unprecedented gathering' convened by the United Nations. The United Millennium Summit gave birth to a dream in which our nations promised to slash extreme poverty by half by the year 2015. These promises contained eight wide but measurable goals by which the preventable indignity endured by over a billion people would be brought to an end.

This covenant with our extreme poor came to be known as the Millennium Development Goals (MDGs). The MDGs were more than fiscal promises to the poor. This was a historic and moral contract to 'spare no effort . . . freeing the entire human race from want.'[5]

Christians who were already fully committed to the alleviation of poverty and who had stepped up to the plate as full partners in global movements such as Jubilee 2000 and Make Poverty History felt that these promises resonated with the spirit of the Old Testament prophets and the teachings of Jesus. And the growing impulse to respond to the poor which was growing steadily across many sections of the evangelical church felt a call to respond to the MDGs. Micah Challenge is that response.

MICAH CHALLENGE

Launched in October 2004, Micah Challenge now has some forty national campaigns. Our vision is of a world free from extreme poverty. Our aim is to establish a global movement to encourage deeper Christian commitment to the poor and hold governments to account for their pledge to halve world poverty by 2015. Our mission is to be a global voice on poverty for Christians, encouraging Christians to learn about the issues, find ways to reach out and help the poor, and to fight for justice.

Micah Challenge is distinct as a coalition of Christians with a global reach of 420 million evangelical Christians in 128 nations; we have been mandated by 300 relief and development agencies and 129 Evangelical Alliances to advocate on the MDGs. And the campaign in its present form will stop in 2015.

In our prayers and personal actions, our letters and lobbying we are governed by the penetrating question from the prophet Micah: 'And what does the LORD require of you? To act justly and to love mercy and to walk humbly with your God' (Mic. 6:8).

The Millennium Development Goals are invitations to act – not just talk. They are not perfect tools; world poverty needs an even more radical response. And we know that there is a great danger that they can lead us into what Martin Luther King Jr called the 'paralysis of analysis'. But nothing else gives us as comprehensive a yardstick by which to hold ourselves accountable, or provides the universal language with which to talk about maternal deaths or a global response to reducing and reversing HIV/AIDS. When I spoke to medical workers in a remote village in Zambia they told me that these were useful benchmarks by which to evaluate their battle against infant mortality and maternal deaths. And when I spoke to the Prime Minister of Australia last October, he spoke the same language.

But our starting point is not the MDGs: we are involved in this work because we are on a mission. The arrogance of the church is to suppose that we bring God's mission to an unsuspecting and disinterested world. But mission is invariably God's response to the pain of a world which, as the apostle Paul would tell us, is often groaning in expectation of a response from us.

As Chris Wright, Langham Partnership's International Director, once said: 'the church doesn't have a mission, but God has a mission for the church.'[6]

There is enough for all. The earth is a generous mother; she will provide in plentiful abundance food for all her children if they will but cultivate her soil in justice and in peace.
Bourke Cockran[40]

33

BIBLE:
YOUR
KINGDOM
COME

KRISH KANDIAH

Someone once defined politics as 'the art of swallowing frogs and looking like you are enjoying them'[7] I am often reminded of that definition as I see politicians interviewed by the likes of Jeremy Paxman. As awkward questions are fired machine-gun style by the unrelenting interviewer, the politicians have to wear those thin fake smiles and look good for the camera. It can often seem as though they are adopting a thin veneer of respectability to disguise a cesspool of power-mongering and scheming. It all gives the impression that politics is about looking good while being bad.

Politics has been turned upside down by the media seeking scandal stories that grab the headlines and the ratings. And the word 'spin' has entered not just the political vocabulary but everyday parlance as a way of finding a good angle on a bad situation. It is no wonder that people are losing faith in politics. But before we decide that Christianity and politics don't mix, we must take note that Jesus' teaching was intrinsically political.

The Sermon on the Mount begins with some radical messages that would have shocked the politicians and the populace alike. Jesus taught that the kingdom belonged to the poor, the pure, the

> I passionately believe that if we are to see God's justice reign on the earth it starts with action. We must take this cause to end human trafficking into our communities, to the media, to the lawmakers of our country and to the very heart of government.
>
> Ben Cooley, Founder and CEO of Hope for Justice

peacemakers and the persecuted, not the pious, the proficient, the prosperous or the power-mongers. He raised the bar far above legislation in challenging people's motives when it came to cases of murder, adultery and divorce. He commanded his followers to love even their enemies from their hearts and to give to the needy out of a generous spirit. This was a message that would transform society and herald God's kingdom. And, so we didn't miss the point, Jesus taught us to pray a timeless political prayer.

The Lord's Prayer (Matt. 6:9–13) first of all reminds us to acknowledge that God is the King of the universe. From the tiniest ant to the highest mountain, each molecule, every constellation is his; there is nothing that God does not have the right to rule over. If we restrict God and his influence just to our personal devotions, or just to our church meetings, or just to our private family life, we demonstrate that we have not understood his reign. When we pray to our holy Father in heaven (v. 9), we pledge allegiance to him and declare him to be the ruler over every aspect of our lives, our communities and our world.

Secondly, every time we pray 'your kingdom come, your will be done' (v. 10) we are praying a prayer of political agitation. We are proclaiming that we are not content with the way things are being run, and that we want God's government to be fully expressed here, as it is in heaven. Whether we are concerned about our children being bullied at school, or our taxes being fairly administered, or our hospitals being properly funded, or our charity donations helping those suffering from malnutrition, or our soldiers being safe in action, by praying this prayer we are vocalizing what we long for on earth – peace, justice, righteousness and compassion.

Thirdly, the Lord's Prayer recognizes that whatever is going on around us in the political sphere, ultimately it is God who will hold us to account for our choices, whether to do evil or to show forgiveness, and that it is God who will ultimately provide for our needs. We may think that our bread comes from Tesco, and that the government should ensure that it remains affordable, but at the end of the day we look to our good King who rules over the weather, the crops, the rulers and the distributors, to meet our most basic of needs (v. 11).

The Lord's Prayer does not ask that we get teleported off the planet when the going gets tough, nor is it an ejector seat out of the nitty-gritty of life on earth. Instead it is a prayer that seeks God's power to be demonstrated in the here and now. We are told to ask not for pie in the sky when we die, but for God's rule here where we live. Politics and faith can walk hand in hand, when they serve God's kingdom here on earth.

One day the trees went out to anoint a king for themselves. They said to the olive tree, 'Be our king.' But the olive tree answered, 'Should I give up my oil, by which both gods and men are honoured, to hold sway over the trees?' Next, the trees said to the fig-tree, 'Come and be our king.' But the fig-tree replied, 'Should I give up my fruit, so good and sweet, to hold sway over the trees?' Then the trees said to the vine, 'Come and be our king.' But the vine answered, 'Should I give up my wine, which cheers both gods and men, to hold sway over the trees?' Finally all the trees said to the thornbush, 'Come and be our king.'

Judges 9:8–14

But justice is a higher standard. Africa makes a fool of our idea of justice; it makes a farce of our idea of equality. It mocks our pieties; it doubts our concern, and it questions our commitment. Six and a half thousand Africans are still dying every day of preventable, treatable disease, for lack of drugs we can buy at any drug store. This is not about charity: This is about Justice and Equality.

Bono[38]

Section 2:

JUST POLITICS AND DEMONSTRATING INTEGRITY

THREE POLITICIANS
TALK ABOUT INTEGRITY

KRISH KANDIAH: How do you reconcile being a politician and being a Christian?

STEVE WEBB

Some of the biggest things I care about are issues of global justice and poverty, and although there are things that individuals can do, actually governance can either work with the grain of that, or thwart it. In my case, I felt I was doing what I could as a Christian in supporting charities such as Tearfund and Christian Aid, and then in the 1980s I found that it was all offset by a government that was cutting aid budgets to the extent of the entire spending of all the agencies put together. So I wasn't changing anything or making the impact I wanted to make by standing on the sidelines as a private individual. I needed to be in the decision-making process, applying my values and my priorities.

There wasn't a perfect fit 'Steve Webb Party', and if there was I'm not sure I would have joined it! But having made the choice to become a Lib Dem, based on finding people I respected, over the years I have found that what they stand for fits me better and better. Broadly speaking, the Lib Dem Party fitted my worldview, shared my values and, although I might not be comfortable with everything in the manifesto, since it isn't ever a finished article, I hope that I, as a Christian, can help shape it.

> I believe Christians should be actively involved in politics to ensure that policies reflect Christian values of Social Justice, Compassion, Respect for life, Stewardship of resources, Empowerment and Reconciliation. Join a political party, influence the outcome, shape the agenda and challenge the status quo.
>
> Ram Gidoomal, Businessman, Social Entrepreneur and Author

GARY STREETER

I believe that politics is about getting into office so you can put your principles into practice to help people to change things. I profoundly believe that only a real encounter with Jesus Christ can impact human nature, but in a pluralistic culture, most people won't have that encounter. Human nature is deeply flawed and fallen, and people are not going to work for their country or some great state organization, as the Russians found out, but they will work for themselves and their family and, by harnessing that creative self-interest, we can generate wealth as well as spend it, without taxing people to death and adding bureaucratic burdens to business. I also believe that most people are trying to be constructive and good and take responsibility for their society. As a Christian Conservative, I would like to cut with the grain to put in place a system that helps people to do what they do best or most naturally and live up to their God-given potential. We need law and order because there is always the minority who want to destroy and bring down, but most people want to live in a positive community, a flourishing family and a strong nation.

Coming out of the back of the Thatcher years, we got ourselves horribly lost and stuck in a time warp, but under David Cameron, the Conservative Party has retained our heritage, dusted off some old principles such as compassion, renewed our interest in internationalism, and added a cutting edge in a changing landscape. The party's long, deep heritage of values and principles which I firmly hold to – supporting entrepreneurs, family and nation – enable us to help individuals to make free choices to create wealth for the community around them. It is this individual responsibility and freedom of choice to access all God has done for us that I see is the broad thrust of the gospel, the crux of my personal faith and the core of the Conservative Party ethos.

ANDY REED

Whereas the Conservative worldview will take any problem and always start with the individual or entrepreneurs, my Christian faith draws me to the Labour view, which tends to be more co-operative and collaborative. I don't believe that the market is good – it has winners and losers, it needs regulation and price mechanisms, it can't always deliver what it promises and it can therefore be bad. Similarly, my view is that individual self-interest will not always necessarily create the common good either. My clarion call is Micah 6:8, which challenges us to do more than just think about justice; we also need to 'act justly and to love mercy' as well as 'walk humbly' – not seeking recognition for it. You can't do all that as individuals; you need to have a collective sense of responsibility.

The Early Church is my model for society; it was not about creating wealth, but about sharing it. The Early Church was known as the Way (see Acts 9:2) because it demonstrated a way of life. I would counter-argue that our heritage is twisted because materially we have done well largely on the back of diamonds and gold and raw materials from Africa, which allowed us to industrialize. This prosperity often twists our understanding of the gospel as our wealth is not created, but loaned to us temporarily. If we are genuinely following Jesus in discipleship, then we should be looking to create a world that is based on the values of the Early Church. That doesn't put me in the old-fashioned model of socialism that sits in London and takes over large parts of British industry. I am a co-operative Member of Parliament because I believe that small co-operatives that give the sense of localism and individualism and collective responsibility are the most successful, as the level of bureaucracy is in touch with the outcome and the community. I recognize the roles of individuals, like Steve and Gary, but I want to put it into a collective sense at the same time. I would argue that we have more responsibilities as a collective not only locally, but nationally and globally. Our actions affect our neighbours and with a world ever more intertwined, our neighbours are those 6 billion of us around the world made in God's image.

For the LORD is righteous, he loves justice; upright men will see his face.

Psalm 11:7

43

STEVE WEBB

For me, the most amazing thing about the gospel is that God gave us the freedom to reject his Son, and knew that we would and let us do it anyway. There must be something extraordinary about the dignity and the value of an individual and their choice and responsibility if the almighty, perfect God can give us that freedom, knowing that all of us would choose wrongly. If we had no choice, we would all be slaves, not heirs of the kingdom. Because of this freedom, I am nervous of using the power of the state to coerce people into Christian values or promote our faith, just as I would be uncomfortable if another faith was dominant and structures were in place to impose their beliefs. God gave us a framework and guidelines, but fundamentally we are free. Likewise, the state has to set boundary lines, but should always, in my view, presume to let people be morally responsible agents. I also believe that you shouldn't vote for someone just because they are Christian, as Christians can hold some very diverse views about what their faith means on issues of justice, so I would recommend to people to vote on issues that really matter and look for candidates who hold strongly to those issues. What I like about the Liberal Democrats is the coherent worldview, allowing individuals to have power over their own lives, decentralizing power and responsibility, with an instinct to side with individuals and marginalized, and with a concern for justice and fairness. To me, a concern for individual fairness, and international compassion are the central tenets of my faith; these I can work for in the political arena.

KRISH KANDIAH: Coming from these different positions, how do you relate to one another? How can you be both adversaries in the House and brothers in the faith?

STEVE WEBB

I have never been a very 'tribal' politician, and believe that there are good people in all the political parties. For me, it would be incredible to say that I would not work with another member of the body of Christ simply because they had a different party political label. Just because we may have different views on the working of the economy or the role of the state does not mean we cannot work together in an atmosphere of mutual trust and respect, and I think that this is something that the public wants to see in its political representatives.

> The devil led him up to a high place and showed him in an instant all the kingdoms of the world. And he said to him, 'I will give you all their authority and splendour, for it has been given to me, and I can give it to anyone I want to. So if you worship me, it will all be yours.' Jesus answered, 'It is written: "Worship the Lord your God and serve him only."'
>
> Luke 4:5–8

ANDY REED

Despite our real differences, at the end of the day we are all Christians and we have a strong overlap as we all want to serve God's purposes in the world and in our work. For this reason, Christians from all parties come together regularly to pray. We have also formed a cross-party group of Christian MPs – the G6 – to imagine what Britain may look like in 2020, and to come up with a common Christian vision and response. Parliamentarians and the media have a pretty good idea of what Christians are *against*, but very little about what we are *for*. Our hope is that we can help church leaders, parliamentarians and others to understand that Christians have something positive to add to the debate. The reason we can come together and write this book is because of the trust and fellowship that we have built up over the past twelve years in the G6.

GARY STREETER

The G6 is a great support for Christian MPs. I think of myself as 'church' first, and involved in politics second. So when people say that although we have some Christian politicians the church isn't involved in shaping politics, this is a contradiction. Church, in the form of Christian MPs from all parties and their supporters and advisers and voters, is making a difference. The Conservative Party has transformed its policy in the last fifteen years on social justice, parenting and compassion issues, and that has been driven almost entirely by the church in terms of Christian MPs, activists and party members, challenging and probing from the inside and moving the party significantly on the whole domestic agenda. There is a role for the pulpit – the church speaking out – a role for individual engagement and a role for the nationally organized campaign and together we can change the wind.

KRISH KANDIAH: Have your beliefs and your work ever come into conflict? How do you handle the frustrations of the job and the divisive issues of the day?

STEVE WEBB

Regarding the traditional moral issues such as abortion and euthanasia, this is usually free vote territory and most of the time I do not feel that I am constantly wrestling with my conscience or being dragged through legislation against my will. Usually I am voting on technicalities, and if I don't have time to get my head round all of them in every area, I trust my colleagues who share my broad values and who scrutinize the technical details, and are there to guide me. I use the word 'trust' deliberately, because often the presumption is that it is all bullying and coercion, but I am relieved to be able to work together with my party on most issues.

We'll be much better ambassadors for Christ in the political arena is we're filled with the power of love rather than the love of power. Andy Croft

ANDY REED

When we decided to go to war in Iraq I was against it; I was in the minority, and I felt torn. Although a million people marched into London on Saturday 15 February 2003 with a petition, polls were telling the government that 56 per cent of Britain felt we should go to war. My faith and my work came into conflict and I felt I couldn't remain in my role as a Parliamentary Private Secretary, so I resigned on a matter of conscience.

GARY STREETER

The MP expense scandal has been another wake-up call for Christians but I believe it will strengthen us in the end. It is easy to develop complacency instead of integrity and compassion and prayer and wisdom. If politics is sleazy, then we need people in politics who seek the eternal perspective of God's wisdom, who are not self-serving, but prepared to make unpopular decisions that affect the poor, the vulnerable and the elderly. I am the only Conservative MP who has ever been to North Korea, for example, and it was shocking to see the people there grim, cold, scared, oppressed and hungry while in South Korea they have food, freedom, better jobs and roofs over their heads. It isn't perfect, but the enormous difference comes down to politics. They were once the same country and the same people with the same conditions. This shows how important politics is, and so I have to get involved despite the sleaze and scandals.

A DAY IN THE LIFE OF . . .
ANDY REED MP

Re-elected as vice chair of Christians in parliament all party group at AGM (9 hours ago)

Supporting Breast Cancer Awareness event (7 hours ago)

Wore it pink to help publicize and beat breast cancer. Photos later! (7 hours ago)

Really useful meeting with BISL and discussions based on the importance of the sport & leisure industry to the economy (6 hours ago)

Good to see IGD report shows recession is not stopping the growth of ethical shopping for goods & services. Britain most ethical in Europe! (5 hours ago)

In Health Questions but looking unlikely to get called. Wanted to raise issues from Carers Conference I attended last week in Lboro (4 hours ago)

Speaker kindly let me in to ask about quality of care. Carers were really upset by some of the standards they witness. Often needs humanity (4 hours ago)

Long tribute to those killed in Afghanistan makes the rest of PMQs seem a little meaningless. Perhaps we should spend time reflecting (3 hours ago)

Useful meeting at the Treasury with Digital Minister Stephen Timms (6 mins ago)

SPEAKER'S CORNER: LESSONS FROM THE MEDIA

CHARIS GIBSON

'It was *The Sun* Wot Won It'. Never shy of promoting itself, Britain's most popular daily newspaper displayed no doubt in regards to its influence on the Labour election victory in its 1997 headline – and it was equally cocky in predicting the impact its coverage would have when it defected back to blue in 2009.

Sure enough, a MORI poll of *Sun* readers' votes did show a swing from Conservative to Labour in 1997. Whether those readers really took voting instructions from a red-top, or if *The Sun* jumped ship to reflect the already-existing frustrations of its readership, there is undoubtedly a close relationship between the media and our political thinking.

So how can we be aware of the part the media plays on our judgement in the run-up to an election?

No matter what medium you get your news from, the story will have been through a number of filters before it gets to you – from the agenda of a publication to the news editor's decision about whether the story is interesting enough to make the bulletin.

Most British newspapers have clearly defined political agendas. The *Mirror*, *Guardian* and *Observer* traditionally lean toward more left-wing politics, *The Times* usually sits on the left of the fence, *The Independent* is liberal, the *Mail* and *Express* are right-wing and the 'Torygraph' hasn't got its nickname for nothing.

Often, we will naturally reach for the publications whose values we most identify with, and their stories are likely to reinforce or strengthen our own opinions.

For instance, if you regularly read stories about immigration running out of control (e.g. the *Express*), your feelings about immigration policy are likely to be very different than if your daily read dismisses such opinions as wide of the mark (e.g. *The Guardian*).

Unlike the press, television and radio stations in the UK have a duty to be politically impartial. This was the main argument used by the BBC to justify BNP leader Nick Griffin's appearance on *Question Time* in 2009 – but the fact that the majority of the programme focused on picking apart Griffin's views shows that this does not mean every politician will be treated objectively on TV.

Of course, many of us are now turning to the internet for our news. While the same principles as their print and broadcast versions generally apply for online content from the main news providers, bloggers and citizen journalists are not bound by impartiality laws

> **When I give food to the hungry they call me a saint. But when I ask why the poor have no food, they call me a communist**
> Helder Camara[28]

51

> Justice is conscience, not a personal conscience but the conscience of the whole of humanity. Those who clearly recognize the voice of their own conscience usually recognize also the voice of justice. Alexander Solzhenitsyn[36]

or the political allegiances of their bosses. They can be as biased as they like – and there is also no requirement on them to be accurate.

So, while reading blogs is a great way of getting different perspectives on a political debate, it's good to be aware that they are not the most reliable sources of information.

And as you're thinking about where to place your vote, it might be worth picking up a paper or blog you would never normally read, or switching over to a programme you have never watched before. It might not change the way you vote, but it will give you a fuller picture of who you're voting for.

CASE STUDY:
CHURCHES AGAINST POVERTY

We had a few credit cards and a loan but my husband, Tony, had a well-paid job so we could afford them. Then Tony got ill. It was awful and he was laid off work. I had to reduce my hours to look after Tony because he was so ill. Then the bills started coming but we just couldn't pay. I tried phoning the mortgage company to explain, but all they said was, 'If you can't pay, we'll kick you out of your house.' If we tried to talk about debt it would always turn into an argument. It was a complete nightmare, I felt as though I would burst under the pressure. The worst thing is that people don't believe you're on the edge. You know you can't afford a loaf of bread, but people think you're lying. Some weeks we couldn't even afford bread and milk. If I couldn't afford food, we lived on tea and sugar to fill us up.

What sort of initiatives would it take to lift Carol and Tony out of poverty?

Who could they turn to for help?

How would your church support people like Carol and Tony?

Visit the 'Christians Against Poverty' website to see how their lives have been transformed: www.capuk.org/reallifestories

For more information on Christians Against Poverty and to see how you could get involved, visit www.capuk.org.

Christianity and other world faiths have a vital part to play in reaching out to help the poor and marginalized – and reminding those of us in government of our special responsibilities to men, women and children affected by poverty. The values of Christian belief emphasize compassion, generosity and social responsibility. These values strike a chord with our desire to see a world that is just and fair, and free from poverty.

Gordon Brown[46]

Dear PM,

Poverty is a massive problem in the UK today: low incomes, poor housing and growing financial inequality are ripping our communities apart. If you allow the re-growth of huge unjust bonuses in the banking world then our society will fragment further. But that is just one face of poverty. Because we also have a poverty of relationships where families continue to be ravaged by the tyranny of personal choice and our 'whatever' generation. Government must do all they can to prevent family breakdown. We also have the poverty of identity with epidemic levels of depression and self harm blighting lives of our young.

Prime Minister, throw real weight behind those who are healing our communities in practical ways. Those who have real hope for people, based not on what they earn but on their real value. Work with the churches and the community organizations who have a vision of a future where people and the places where they live are marked with wholeness and justice. We can do it together.

Jon Kuhrt

Dear Prime Minister

Please be assured of my prayers for your family and your leadership of this country. I hope that you will find wisdom and revelation for your task in a regular, sustained engagement with the Word of God. God may not be interested in politics (as we humanly understand it), but you can be assured that he is very, very interested in government. To the Lord, government is primarily about the right ordering of our relational priorities. As such, it is the family business of the Father, Son and Holy Spirit. 'Righteousness exalts a nation, but sin is a [disgrace] to a people' (Proverbs 14: 34), and we need God to govern. When Solomon prayed for 'wisdom to govern', God responded with extravagant blessing. This shows his heart for those who heed the call to serve and lead in high office. Please be encouraged to know that the Lord blesses all those who seek to govern – and that includes you. I hope that your term of leadership will be a happy one that brings hope, righteousness and justice. May the joy of the Lord be your strength.

Yours,
Dave Landrum

@TweettothenewPM Welcome to no.10. Amid the glitz and glamour of meeting world leaders don't forget the call and commission of meeting the world's poor. **Andy Frost**

I am involved in politics as an ordinary person that does my bit! I vote, I campaign and I help encourage others to make their voice heard. Martin Luther King inspires me because he demonstrated that change is possible when ordinary people take their cause peacefully to the streets. I believe that as Christians we are called to be peacemakers, called to care for the marginalized and the oppressed, and called to love our neighbours. If we want to see God's values become reality and impact policy, we must therefore enter politics and each person needs to play their part. The Fair Trade movement has been a great example of how Christians have taken seriously a God-given value and made it a practical issue. It is amazing to see how mainstream companies are now changing their tack.

Andy Frost, Director of Share Jesus International

FACTFILE: TOP TEN WAYS FOR CHURCHES TO GET INVOLVED

1 Spend a month in sermons and home groups looking at how the church as a whole and as individual members can impact their local community. One helpful resource for doing this is the 'Square Mile' resource available from the Evangelical Alliance (www.eauk.org/squaremile).

2 Profile local, national and global issues regularly by informing, praying and encouraging involvement.

3 Be active in meeting practical and spiritual needs in your community.

4 Gather together the local church leaders to work co-operatively, and let your MP know the positive steps that are being taken.

5 Pray specifically and publicly for the local MPs and issues they are facing. Invite them to your services.

6 Organize a local hustings (an opportunity for the local candidates to publicly answer questions and explain their vision) before any election and ask tough questions about justice at all levels.

7 Support church members involved in politics in various ways – interview them in front of the church, or for the church magazine; visit them, pray for them.

8 Don't promote one particular party from the pulpit – but encourage everybody to vote, to pray and possibly to join a political party of their choice.

9 Take a lead in promoting social justice issues – by buying fairly traded products, reducing energy bills and paper use, by sharing resources etc.

10 Include books on your bookstall that seek to grapple with issues of faith and politics. (See Appendix 1.)

> The voluntary sector, including the churches and faith communities have always played a significant role in social action in Britain – in education, in welfare, in support for so many of the most vulnerable and needy in our society. Virtually every community in the country benefits from your work in some way.
>
> Tony Blair[31]

SPEAKER'S CORNER: SANCTITY OF LIFE

LYNDON BOWRING

The most important aspect of being human is that each of us has been created in the image of God himself. Genesis 1 describes how God made everything and saw that 'it was good'. But the pinnacle finally came when 'God created [human beings] in his own image, in the image of God he created . . . them' (Gen. 1:27). The human race was placed in charge of everything else – commissioned to rule over the planet and all that is in it as God's representatives here on earth. This makes human life very special and sacred.

In addition is the awesome truth that the Son of God became a human himself, growing from a tiny embryo inside his mother Mary for nine months – just like any other baby. Tragically, in many parts of the world the hallowed protection of a woman's womb has become statistically the most dangerous place to be because of the millions of abortions that are performed. In the UK each year 200,000 pregnancies are terminated – voiceless, innocent victims who, through no fault of their own, never see the light of day or have the opportunity to live out their lives.

The first person to recognize Christ's presence here on earth was Elizabeth's unborn child John, who leapt in the womb when his mother greeted the pregnant Mary. If asked, 'When did Jesus become human?' would we say something like 'Fourteen days after implantation'? The Bible is clear that at the moment the Holy Spirit came upon Mary, Life began within her. Human life is surely sacred right from conception.

You can measure how civilized a society is by looking at how it treats the most vulnerable. Unborn, newly born and disabled children, sick and elderly people all deserve protection and care because they share with us the imprint of God's image. He who gives us life also takes it away at the appointed time and Christians who believe this should speak out wherever necessary. When politicians and the media begin to promote euthanasia as a compassionate and pragmatic approach to people struggling with crippling illnesses and pain, we need to counter the argument. Britain has pioneered palliative treatment and hospice care which offers a much better alternative to giving up hope altogether.

I long to hear more sermons about abortion, euthanasia and other sanctity of life issues as they are far more than political hot potatoes. As humans made in God's image, we have a solemn duty to be messengers and purveyors of life and need to understand the theological reasons behind this conviction.

I quote my friend Revd Dr Nigel Cameron: 'Only when the glory of God is at the beginning and the end and we find our high place just under God, will human dignity flourish – ideas of human rights, sanctity of life, care of the weak all arise from this fact: that we are made in his image, space-time models of God himself in his very image.'

To get involved, why not sign up for CARE's mailing list, which will let you know when these issues are being debated in parliament and how to pray (www.care.org.uk)? Write to the media when they undermine the sanctity of life; support medical and nursing professionals in your church who are facing tough calls on a daily basis; consider joining a political party or standing as a local councillor; think about helping out a hospice near you (www.helpthehospices.org.uk); and, find out if there is a Christian pregnancy counselling centre in your area that you can support (www.careconfidential.com).

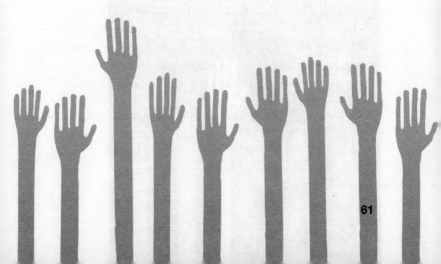

I did not see a temple in the city, because the Lord God Almighty and the Lamb are its temple. The city does not need the sun or the moon to shine on it, for the glory of God gives it light, and the Lamb is its lamp. The nations will walk by its light, and the kings of the earth will bring their splendour into it. On no day will its gates ever be shut, for there will be no night there. The glory and honour of the nations will be brought into it. Nothing impure will ever enter it, nor will anyone who does what is shameful or deceitful, but only those whose names are written in the Lamb's book of life.

Revelation 21:22–27

BIBLE:
KING
OF
THE
JEWS?

KRISH KANDIAH

The ushers appeared to be very keen to have a 'person of colour' seated in full camera shot. So it was I found myself seated right behind Republican presidential candidate John McCain during his final rally before polling day. My friend, who had VIP tickets for the event due to his tireless hours campaigning on the phone, sat next to me on the runway of Indianapolis airport in the hot November sunshine. On my other side was a girl who told me very clearly that as a Christian she felt that McCain's views on abortion, homosexuality and gun rights were closer to the Bible's than the other candidate's. It occurred to me that Jesus' 'big three' were more likely to be justice, truth and compassion, and I found it hard to reconcile that Christians felt morally obligated to vote based solely on issues that were not central to Jesus' message.

The next day I was in Chicago, Barack Obama's home town, as the votes came in. This time I was sitting in the park with a primarily black audience watching the action on the JumboTron TV screens. There was a buzz in the air and loud cheers as state after state declared itself Democrat. When victory was announced, I witnessed the historic moment as the whole city came outside and people were literally dancing on the streets. One guy told me, 'I never thought it would happen in my lifetime, that a black man would be the president of America.' The Christians admitted they had voted Democrat not just because he promised justice for issues relating to Guantanamo Bay, or because of his promises to help the poor, but because he promised change.

But change is an elusive promise. Change is inevitable whichever party has power, and change is not always for the better. I once attended a political rally in Albania when presidential candidate Sali Berisha promised a crowded student campus that 'With us, everything will be much better': he promised better roads, better schools, better hospitals, better everything. It was during his term in office that Albanians lost a billion dollars of their life savings in a 'get rich quick' con the government seemed to have been complicit in. When everyone realized they had lost their money, anarchy broke out. No one could deny there was change, some things even got better, but for most people in the poorest country of Europe there was financial disaster.

Oratory prowess, propaganda and promises typically accompany political rise to power. But in Jesus' last port of call before voting day he produces none of these. In the election between the healer and teacher Jesus, and the terrorist and thief Barabbas, Jesus is silent, the crowds and chief priests vote Barabbas, and the only propaganda around belongs to Pilate, who adds his own postscript to the story: 'JESUS OF NAZARETH, THE KING OF THE JEWS' (John 19:19).

Jesus' death was a political execution. Because of the Roman occupation, the religious leaders couldn't execute Jesus in Jerusalem, so they had to convince the Roman Procurator, Pontius Pilate, to pronounce sentence. Pilate was not interested in

> **This is what the LORD says: 'Maintain justice and do what is right, for my salvation is close at hand and my righteousness will soon be revealed.'**
>
> Isaiah 56:1

arbitrating what he saw as a petty religious disagreement, so the religious leaders made it Pilate's problem by arguing that Jesus' message had major political ramifications that would undercut even the Emperor Caesar's jurisdiction. Jesus' enemies spoke better than they knew.

The cross itself was a piece of political propaganda. The very method of execution that the Romans employed was designed to underline the might of the Empire, by exposing the weakness of their enemies. By stripping the victims, hoisting them up in public and deliberately engineering a long and painful death, the Romans made it very clear that resistance was futile.

And for the final nail in the coffin, Pilate's last piece of propaganda was a multilingual message nailed to the cross proclaiming Jesus to be the 'King of the Jews'. Had Pilate noticed something transcendent in the man that had challenged him to recognize that only God had the real power in the universe? Or was Pilate drawing attention to the powerlessness of any who tried to stake a claim against him and the Roman authorities he represented? Was he making a fool of Jesus, or the Jews, or the judicial system? Was he trying to excuse himself for the execution of God himself?

Whatever his motive, Pilate ended up popular with the Jewish leaders and the crowds on the street. We are also told that on that day Herod and Pilate became friends after a history of antagonism (Luke 23:12). It was in opposition to Jesus that the figureheads of power in Israel were united. Power based on conspiracy, corruption and propaganda often seems to do very well for itself for a while, but ultimately the flawed system will crack. The Roman Empire, after years of trying to eradicate Jesus' followers, eventually bowed to the gospel when Emperor Constantine was converted. Berisha was forced to flee the country he had ruled after misleading the Albanian people with his promises of financial prosperity. On the other hand, power based on integrity may seem unpopular, but it will stand the test of time. Jesus did not end up a corpse crucified under a cartoon caption. When he rose from the dead he showed that all powers are ultimately accountable to a just and perfect God.

George Bell, the Bishop of Chichester during the Second World War, was friends with Christian leaders in Germany who opposed the Nazi regime. Bell took up the cause of his Christian brothers who were imprisoned and in danger of execution, publicly condemning their mistreatment, as well as the persecution of the Jews. But Bell's voice not only spoke out against the Nazi corruption. He publicly criticized Winston Churchill and Arthur Harris, the Air Chief Marshall responsible for the carpet bombing of Dresden, where non-combatants and innocent civilians were the primary targets. Bell was very unpopular at the time, but he followed a Master who was willing to speak the truth whatever the cost.

Integrity in politics may mean, like Jesus, we refuse to play the propaganda prowess game. It may mean we shy away from making promises we can't guarantee to keep; it may mean we end up the butt of other people's jokes. Some people use Jesus' silence before Pilate to argue that we shouldn't discuss or engage in politics at all, but Jesus broke his silence to challenge Pilate to recognize who he was accountable to. It is in this way that all Christians can engage in politics with integrity as we call the government to account to a higher power, and as we proclaim the truth – no matter what the cost.

Then I saw a new heaven and a new earth, for the first heaven and the first earth had passed away, and there was no longer any sea. I saw the Holy City, the new Jerusalem, coming down out of heaven from God, prepared as a bride beautifully dressed for her husband. And I heard a loud voice from the throne saying, 'Now the dwelling of God is with men, and he will live with them. They will be his people, and God himself will be with them and be their God. He will wipe every tear from their eyes. There will be no more death or mourning or crying or pain, for the old order of things has passed away.'

Revelation 21:1–4

Section 3:

JUST POLITICS AND FINDING INSPIRATION

THREE POLITICIANS TALK ABOUT THE FUTURE

KRISH KANDIAH: As Christians, we want to be thinking beyond who wins the next election. What do you think about the short-termism of politics, and what do you think are going to be the big challenges facing politics of the future?

ANDY REED

Politicians are criticized for trying to win the daily headlines, but although there are a few at the centre of all parties who play that game, behind the scenes there are also deep thinkers concerned for the long-term. There are lots of examples I can give illustrating the investment in the medium-long term. Our commitment to Sure Start is the best way to guarantee the chances of our young children getting to university in eighteen years' time. The Millennium Development Goals are looking much further than the next election. We are setting targets for the Climate Change Act that are looking to the year 2050. We are also talking at the moment about the pension crisis of 2050 and about raising the retirement age. The criticism can be levied that if we set the goals beyond our own working careers, are we going to be responsible for them, and will

> # Politics is based on the indifference of the majority. James Reston[27]

anyone hold us accountable for those decisions? Nevertheless, we are thinking ahead, and this offers a challenge to the church. That politics is only focused on the short-term is one of the great myths.

My father retired five years ago from a job that he had gone into when he left school at 16 and left thirty-nine years later. His life had not involved many changes and things seemed pretty certain. Now people live very differently. Travel, communication and distribution have changed beyond recognition even in the last decade or so, and the effect of that has been to turn upside down the world and communities in which we live. The combination of globalization and the pace of change have caused a massive sense of uncertainty about the future. We have mortgages that last for twenty-five years but jobs that can't guarantee us work beyond twelve or twenty-four months if we are lucky. Our financial crisis has called into question the whole consumerist fabric on which we have based much of our life. This 'affluenza' has gone hand in hand with the climate crisis and the recognition that we are living an unsustainable lifestyle. Debt and financial worries are the biggest reason for breakdown in the family – which is the other big challenge for our future – and the reason for much of the current apathy and disillusionment with politics. All these issues have to be addressed, not in a spirit of self-righteousness, but by looking at really meeting people's fundamental needs.

STEVE WEBB

We face a whole raft of problems as we look to the future. Although we think of ourselves as very much an 'island' nation, all the biggest problems we face are global – terrorism, migration, immigration, economy, trade and climate change. Virtually every one of those reflects the fact that we are in an interconnected world and yet I believe we, as a nation, still hold on to the 'empire'. We need to realize the world has changed, our place in it has changed, and that we need to get over our fear of the foreigner and the fear of the unknown. Linked to that we have a changing media role, which is now controlled by rich individuals with their own agendas who can buy daily influence. We also have family breakdown and, on one hand, we are terrified of trying to tell people how to run their lives, but on the other hand, we can't just walk by on the other side of the road while families fall to pieces around us. We need to find a way to address these issues, for the state to engage and be more supportive of strong relationships and good environments for kids to grow up in. This is a real challenge and Christians ought to be right in there with all these issues of national and global justice and poverty.

GARY STREETER

I agree with Steve and Andy that a lot of the issues are international and we are living in an increasingly globalized and globalizing world, although looking back through history, we shouldn't assume that things always go in a straight line and keep on globalizing. There may be a massive rupture of one kind or another and one thing we can certainly say is that the future will have conflict in it! Energy security hasn't been mentioned yet and I think this will be a huge issue as the oil runs out over the next thirty to fifty years. We will not only need to find some replacement energy source, but there is the potential for major powers to fight over the increasingly scarce resources. If we add to that the implications of climate change on the poorest in our world we will see growing issues relating to famine, hunger, displacement and the mass migrations of people. This, I believe, will be a major challenge over the next twenty years.

On the domestic front, I agree that family breakdown will be a serious challenge. Quality of parenting is going to be a huge issue for a significant minority. An increasing number of people growing up in a household of chaos are going to have no idea about how to bring up their own children, unless we intervene in some way – although intervention is complex and difficult. The starfish principle is helpful here. If there are thousands of starfish stranded on the sand and there is no way of rescuing them all, then by simply throwing one starfish back into the sea, we are making a significant impact on that one life. It is in this way that I can see the church being well placed to help.

> The great paradox and humor of God's audacious power: a stuttering prophet will be the voice of God, a barren old lady will become the mother of a nation, a shepherd boy will become their king, and a homeless baby will lead them home. Shane Claibourne[54]

KRISH KANDIAH: So what keeps you going into the future, and who inspires you most?

STEVE WEBB

It is often in dealing with individuals that I get the most job satisfaction because it is so tangible. People come to me usually because they have an intractable problem and nobody else seems to be listening. By going the extra mile for them, I can make a real difference in their lives, which in turn is hugely rewarding for me. Several years ago, I was involved in helping a family who were struggling to adopt from Romania and I went with them to see the Romanian ambassador. This couple were desperate to help a little girl in an orphanage who had been abandoned, unloved and uncared for, but they had come up against regulations due to Romania joining the European Union and legalities preventing families from adopting for all the wrong reasons. This past weekend, I happened to bump into this girl. She is happy, settled in school and part of her new family. Seeing her reminded me of how far we had all come and I felt proud to know that I played a part in that. This is where the reward and inspiration comes from. In a political system where one party has a hefty majority, I can routinely win the argument in any given debate, but then serially lose the vote and this can be soul-destroying. Five years ago, I was told by government that there was no point in campaigning for women pensioners, who on average are very badly off; indeed, they said that it was a terrible idea. But I felt that this was a significant issue, and I did a lot of technical detailed work behind the scenes, through legislative amendments and through the media to gain public sympathy, and finally it is now seen as received wisdom that we do something about this issue, and laws are being changed. Despite the frustrations of not getting credit for that, I know that when I use the two letters after my name to contact the highest level on behalf of my constituents and break through on a problem, or I use the media to influence the climate of public opinion on an issue, and laws eventually get changed, these things inspire me to continue as a political reformer.

ANDY REED

Travelling around the world, I have discovered wonderful Christians in cardboard boxes in the slums in the poorest part of Uganda; in Uzbekistan, I met pastors that were going to prison the next day. We are often taught that it is in adversity that true faith shines out, and when you see that eye to eye with people, you know that these are the genuine heroes, who wouldn't count themselves as such; it is these who are the most influential people, inspiring and humbling me into further action.

Desmond Tutu once said, 'When people tell me that the Bible has nothing to do with politics, then I ask them, which Bible are you talking about?'[8] This is a man who transcended faith and politics in a way that is an inspiration. He couldn't just stand by and watch apartheid or even just philosophize about it – he had to speak out, and I watched that, growing up.

I wanted to change the world as an 18-year-old, but now I have learned to step back and take the long view, and I am inspired in this by the prayer of Archbishop Romero who called us 'prophets of a future not our own'. William Wilberforce is another hero of mine, who not only had a social and campaigning heart but a lot of perseverance. It took forty years of his life to abolish slavery, and he was lucky as he saw the results in his lifetime.

GARY STREETER

After Jesus, who I believe called me into this work, I have also been influenced and inspired by William Wilberforce and Chuck Colson.[9] Colson helped me when I began in politics and was trying to work out why I was here, and I still dip into his books from time to time.

Some years ago, I was powerfully moved by a story told me by Martin Robinson, the National Director of Together in Mission, about a small church in 1900. One evening, the church leaders got together and were feeling rather gloomy about their lack of growth, despite sixty years of Wesley and the Revival, and it was then that they decided to start a different conversation with their communities. They rolled up their sleeves and got stuck into social action and good works without losing anything of the gospel message. Rolling forward the story 100 years later, the church saw massive growth on the back of this social engagement. Wilberforce probably wouldn't have happened without Wesley, and the two together caused a great transformation of church and state; there's an inspiration for us there. I have seen God bring renewal to the church in my lifetime, and now I am seeing God clearly leading us into social engagement, and that is an exciting thing.

I urge, then, first of all, that requests, prayers, intercession and thanksgiving be made for everyone – for kings and all those in authority, that we may live peaceful and quiet lives in all godliness and holiness. This is good, and pleases God our Saviour, who wants all men to be saved and to come to a knowledge of the truth.

1 Timothy 2:1–3

A DAY IN THE LIFE OF . . .
GARY STREETER MP

Arrived Westminster office 7.40 a.m. as per norm, large decaff cappuccino in hand. Turn on laptop & pray before ringing wife & reviewing news

8.30 a.m. Join G6 to share & catch up. Most of us still down re the negativity of the expenses scandal, we encourage each other in a time of prayer

Attack emails until 11 o'clock meeting with fellow MPs to discuss the themes for Prime Minister's Questions for which I have number 11

Manage to ask a question to the Development Secretary about climate change and low lying countries like the Maldives and got a half decent reply

Just got my question in to the PM about fair funding for Devon schools at 12.29 p.m.! In rowdy house the PM's reply completely misses the point

Manage a sandwich lunch in my office while I catch up with more emails; speak to a constituent on the phone with a mouth full of Mars bar

Met up with some charming primary school children to chat about what MPs do. Really enjoy these encounters, the hour flew by

Straight into meeting with Regional Development agency which we will abolish if we win election. Complete waste of time, the 45 mins dragged

Vote at 4 p.m. on opposition motion re compensation for those who lost money from Equitable Life. Then back to emails and further meetings

Vote again at 7 p.m. and then dash for the train going west, hurray. Early start the next day to go campaigning in Cornwall

ORDINARY RADICALS STORY: BEN

Ben was sitting on a beach one day, taking some time out to plan a sermon. Feeling inadequate and uninspired, he called out to God for the right words to say. With just an hour left before the meeting, he was getting desperate, when his thoughts were interrupted by a voice further down the beach shouting for help.

Ben tried harder to focus on his prayers and his preparations, getting increasingly frustrated as the cries for help became more and more urgent.

'Just shut up,' he said. 'I am trying to hear Jesus.'

At that moment God spoke to Ben's heart and said, 'I hope this is not a picture of my church, ignoring the millions of cries for help from people across the earth because they are too busy with their meetings!' As Ben got up to help the man down the beach, he was overwhelmed with conviction for God's heart for the broken and oppressed.

Up until that point in Ben's life, he was working in the music industry, having trained as an opera singer. But this moment changed the course of his life, as he realized that the gospel of Jesus Christ meant he could not ignore the cries for help in our communities.

It was not only God's voice Ben heard that day. He heard the voices of millions trapped in slavery, the voices of two children a minute being sold as commodities, the voices of precious women and

> **This, then, is how you should pray: 'Our Father in heaven, hallowed be your name, your kingdom come, your will be done on earth as it is in heaven.'**
> Matthew 6:9,10

children being brutally raped for profit, and they were voices he could not ignore. In Exodus, the Bible relates how God heard the cries of the people of Israel suffering at the hands of their slave masters, and said to Moses, '. . . now, go. I am sending you' (Exod. 3:10). Similarly, Ben understood the connection between the cries of the people and the vital need to do something about it.

Ben's response was to found an organization called Hope for Justice, which is committed to rescuing trafficked people, restoring lives through rehabilitation and pursuing justice by prosecuting those responsible. Using his musical connections he launched this with an awareness event in 2008 called The Stand at the NEC Arena in Birmingham, which brought together performances from significant bands, well-known speakers and thousands of guests to worship, pray and get involved.

Ben now calls himself an abolitionist, determined to live to see slavery and human trafficking end in his lifetime. He works to raise up a generation who will influence all levels of society, speaking out about the laws being made, and lobbying for legislation to protect vulnerable and abused people in our world. He knows this is a long-haul journey, requiring specialist lawyers, investigators, people who will work to influence the political process, and those who will give their lives to help others they may never meet. He firmly believes that with God, all things are possible.

INTERVIEW
WITH
JON KUHRT

Krish Kandiah: Why do you believe Christians should be actively involved with politics?

JON The key point is to realize that we are involved anyway; we have no choice about being political because if we choose not to engage then it is a vote for the status quo – the way things are. Ken Leech, a vicar who started the homelessness charity Centrepoint said, 'All Christians are political, whether they realize it or not. But especially when they don't realize it'.[10]

Christians need to be involved because we believe in a God who cares passionately about his world and his creation, and consequently how it is run. The Bible is hugely political – in that it is about how God wants people to behave and act towards him, and towards each other. This involves economics and law because these are tools that need to be used to build justice. So often, it is injustice which dominates God's world and this grieves him.

As believers in God we have much to bring to politics – a deeper commitment to justice and compassion which throughout history has made a difference in the political sphere through people like William Wilberforce, Lord Shaftesbury, Elizabeth Fry, Martin Luther King, Desmond Tutu and many, many others.

> When churches started demonstrating on debt, governments listened – and acted. When churches started organizing, petitioning, and even that most unholy of acts today, God forbid, lobbying on AIDS and global health, governments listened – and acted. I'm here today in all humility to say: you changed minds; you changed policy; and you changed the world. So, thank you. Bono[37]

Krish Kandiah: How can Christians get involved?

JON Be involved in your local community – what issues do local people care about? How can you help make a noise about key issues local to you?

How does your church or youth group connect with issues of justice either locally or globally? How can you build knowledge of what is going on and get passionate with others about making a stand?

Join the Christian group of the party that you believe in and be an advocate for Jesus' politics within it. Be brave and courageous – don't just follow the crowd, but be willing to ask the difficult questions.

> 'He will be a spirit of justice to him who sits in judgment, a source of strength to those who turn back the battle at the gate. Isaiah 28:6

Krish Kandiah: Can you give us some examples?

JON I went on a march organized by The Peace Alliance and local churches between Peckham and Brixton following a spate of youth murders in South London. The march deliberately walked across many different gang areas to declare that everyone was one in Christ. We sang Christian songs but it felt much more political than it ever does 'in church'. The march declared God's love into the darkness of violence, pain and anger – giving confidence to the many people within churches trying to make a difference through youth clubs and social action projects.

Another example is the 'Living Wage' campaign organized by London Citizens. They bought shares and attended HSBC's Annual General Meeting and interrupted the chair at the start to raise the issue of how much the cleaners are paid in the bank's building in Canary Wharf. This led to meetings with the 'powers that be' and that in turn led to changes in the wages paid to cleaning staff across Canary Wharf. Many local churches are members of London Citizens, and together they have raised their collective voice on many issues of justice.

Krish Kandiah: Who has most inspired your own activism?

JON The Christian that most inspires me to political action is Christian socialist Bob Holman because he moved from a comfortable position as a lecturer to live on one of the poorest estates in the country, Easterhouse in Glasgow. From this true position of authority, he has campaigned tirelessly for the poor and marginalized – writing articles, books, and changing opinion.

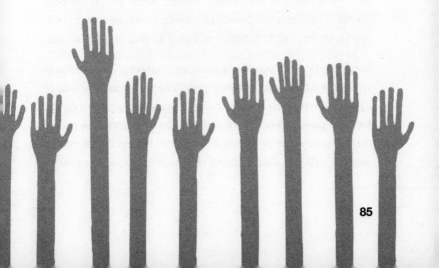

IDIOT'S GUIDE TO . . .
LOCAL ELECTIONS

LAURI MOYLE

Getting involved at local government level can change your area significantly for the good. It is astonishing to realize how much the council actually does that influences the day-to-day life of you and your neighbours. The administration of social justice such as council housing, social services and education is all handled by the council. This means that those people in most need where you live and worship rely on the wisdom and, in many cases, the benevolence of the council for their daily living. The disabled rely on the council to ensure that roads and footpaths are kept in good working order, while local businesses rely on the council to ensure that good parking facilities are available to their clients.

Local government varies depending on where you live. In England, if you live in a large city such as Manchester or London, you will live in a borough or metropolitan district, which will be run by a council. These councils provide all your local services such as local town planning, public transport or library facilities and social care.

If you live in a town, you will have a unitary authority. They provide all local services, but also represent people living in an area outside of that town. In more rural areas, the responsibilities are divided up into two tiers called the county council and district council. The county council is the larger of the two and provides around 80 per cent of services, while the district council provides more localized services.

> # Politics is too serious a matter to be left to politicians. Charles De Gaulle[26]

There are also over ten thousand other, smaller councils which take care of things such as bus stop shelters, public toilets, footpath lighting and waste bins. These councils might be your parish council or community council.

You can find more information about how your local area is governed on the internet, in the library, or at the local town hall or its equivalent.

Each of the councils mentioned above have elected representatives who are unpaid politicians. They are often members of a political party, though they need not be. These men and women come to council meetings and make decisions on behalf of their constituents. Although none of the councillors are paid, they often get small allowances to allow them to fulfil their public duty. They may have a normal day job and after getting back from work, go to council meetings to make decisions about local issues.

Decisions at the local level are usually made by an executive committee that is scrutinized by panels or other committees. Different councillors will sit on different committees so as to be able to focus on specific areas of governance.

Most meetings are open to the public, though only members of the council are usually allowed to talk. A 'forward look plan' outlining when meetings will take place, and what focus they will have, is published in advance. Attending a meeting or two in your area might be a good way for you to get a feel for how things work. Try picking a subject that impacts you, your family and perhaps your church in a significant way. Who knows? Perhaps God will call you to local politics!

I vote because people gave their lives to win the opportunity to vote. We shouldn't take such a privilege for granted. I vote because each vote counts. I vote because I don't have the right to moan about the way things are unless I actively engage and use my vote! Andy Frost

I vote because it's a wonderful privilege to be able to shape politics and government through open elections, and it should not be taken for granted. I vote because we get the government we deserve – we have a duty to care about the shape and nature of our social relations. I vote because it's an opportunity to actually change something – every vote counts.

Dave Landrum, Senior Parliamentary Officer for the Bible Society

I vote because it makes a difference – it actually does decide who's in charge! I vote because who's in charge profoundly affects the poor and socially excluded both here and around the world. I vote because if we don't accept the smaller opportunities to 'have our say', how can we ever accept the bigger ones with integrity? Andy Croft

FACTFILE: TOP TEN REASONS TO VOTE

1 Voting publicly recognizes that we submit to the authority of the political system in our nation as established by God (Rom. 13:1–7).

2 Voting recognizes the equality of all people and their right to speak and be heard (Deut. 10:17–19).

3 Voting is one way that we can obey God's command to seek the good of those around us and our nation as a whole (Jer. 29:7).

4 Voting shows that we care deeply about who our leaders are as we are urged to offer prayer and intercession on their behalf (1 Tim. 2:1,2).

5 Voting is a simple yet significant way we can do something about politics in our nation. 'All that is required for evil to prevail is for good men to do nothing', Edmund Burke (see Ps. 34:14).

6 Voting makes a difference the way a grain of salt makes a difference, and that is how we are to influence our society for good (Matt. 5:13).

7 Voting is a privilege not to be taken for granted. Those of us who reap the benefits of living in a democracy should play a part in upholding the principles of democracy.

8 Not voting is a form of voting, as it will influence the outcome. We need to take responsibility for our actions, as well as our lack of actions (Luke 10:25–37).

9 Voting is part of our stewardship to use all the resources we have been given in ways that honour God; to waste a vote is to squander a gift.

10 Voting is the way we delegate our own responsibility to take care of the planet to others more capable, so we can pursue our own vocation.

SPEAKER'S CORNER: LESSONS FROM THE CREDIT CRUNCH

DONALD HAY

'The financial crisis is over, and we are back to business as usual ...' Wishful thinking, or a justified sigh of relief? It is astonishing how quickly the dark days of 2007–8 are being forgotten: when people queued for hours to withdraw their savings from Northern Rock, when Lehman Brothers filed for bankruptcy in the States, when major UK banks had to be rescued by the taxpayer, and when perfectly sound corporations in manufacturing and services discovered that the banks would no longer lend to finance their business. We are, of course, living with the real consequences in terms of unemployment, negative equity in housing for many, and savings/pension pots which are a fraction of their previous values. But the storm clouds in the financial sector at least appear to have passed over, and are disappearing over the horizon. So now surely is the time for policymakers to take stock. What went wrong, and can we prevent it from happening again?

Let's first remind ourselves of the purpose of financial institutions and markets. They collect savings from those whose current expenditure is less than their income (they are perhaps saving for retirement through a pension scheme), and channel those savings to households who need to borrow to finance house purchases, and to firms for investment in equipment and materials to support production. The aim is to support the real needs and activities of people and firms. The Christian concept of stewardship should be the objective.

In the process of channelling savings, financial institutions bear risk. They accept short-term deposits and lend them long-term, exposing them to the risk of withdrawal of deposits; and it is always possible that borrowers will default. So prudent financial institutions look for ways to reduce and spread risks. Reduction in risks requires a careful appraisal of those who come to them for loans. Risks can be spread by sharing the exposure to particular loans with other financial institutions (the process of 'securitization' of mortgage lending is a case in point), and this reduces the costs of finance. But too much spreading of risk can lead to less care: if the risk can be offloaded to other financial institutions, then careful evaluation of borrowers is no longer worthwhile. This was in essence the problem with the 'subprime' lending in the US housing market. 'Ninja' mortgages were provided to people with 'no income, no job, no assets'. The US housing market, like that in the UK, boomed and then bust, as interest rates rose and the consequences of careless lending policies came home to roost. (Note too, that the spreading of the risks by securitization also spreads the contagion of failure: many leading banks in North America and the UK were participating indirectly in careless lending policies, and probably had not considered appropriately the risk of their exposure.) What is the moral of this story? You don't provide decent housing for the poor by lending them money that they cannot repay. Something else needs to be done. Housing cannot be left entirely to the market.

Other things were happening in financial markets from the 1990s onwards. Part of their genius is the provision of markets for all kinds of securities such as stocks and shares and bonds. This is a good thing as it enables those who need to sell assets to do so quickly and at a price that reflects their value, and equally allows those with money to invest to acquire assets to generate returns over time. But from the 1990s these markets provided the raw material for all sorts of financial wizardry. The hedge funds in particular were able to generate gains from complex trades in these markets, and they achieved astonishing returns on the back of borrowings (it was not unheard of for a hedge fund to borrow 100 times its own capital in order to increase its scale in the markets, so if all went well its returns were increased 100-fold, and equally, if it did not go well, the losses were immense). Underlying all this was the desire for wealth (the bonus culture), and the pursuit of power (the hubris of the quantitative finance people, self referentially 'the masters of the universe'!). What is the moral of this story? The financial sector needs to recall that its fundamental purpose is to serve the productive activity of the economy, and to help consumers to schedule their saving and expenditure over a lifetime.

But it was not all the fault of the financial sector. Consumers were driven by the hope or expectation of future gains in house prices to take on more housing debt: and rising house prices were used as a pretext for borrowing to finance purchases of goods and services. What is the moral of this story? Covetousness became a driving force in the economy, as consumers pursued the illusion of greater happiness derived from larger houses and enhanced spending.

What needs to be done? Much has been written about the need for better regulation: if a financial institution is too big to be allowed to fail, then it definitely needs close attention from the financial authorities to prevent it inflicting losses on everyone else. But perhaps more important is a change in objectives of financial institutions away from wizardry to the fundamentally more important role of supporting the real economy and the needs of households. Finally, we as consumers need to think again about our lifestyles, and the culture of debt on which we have come to rely.

BIBLE:
RENDER
UNTO
CAESAR

KRISH KANDIAH

John Craven looked like he was going to explode. The *Saturday Superstore* children's TV presenter was trying very hard to suppress laughter and surprise as he watched the interviewee squirm. Prime Minister Margaret Thatcher was taking calls from young viewers and one child had asked her bluntly where she would be if a nuclear bomb dropped. Mrs Thatcher launched into a full-scale defence of her nuclear deterrent, to which the tenacious 10-year-old responded, 'But if it did drop, where will you be?' Another salvo of pro-nuclear spending rhetoric was launched at the little girl, who came back for the third time to find out where the Prime Minister's personal nuclear bunker might be located. It was one of those rare occasions when Mrs Thatcher was momentarily flummoxed; finally conceding that she did, in fact, have somewhere she could hide if her policies failed and the unthinkable happened.

The religious and political leaders of Jesus' day might have enjoyed asking that girl for lessons in asking awkward questions. They were constantly trying to trap Jesus into saying something illegal so that they could have an excuse to dismiss and destroy him. One time they asked him a question about taxes, a subject that many political leaders throughout the centuries have been caught out over. In those days the Romans were brutalizing the Jewish people, charging exorbitant taxes for the privilege of living in their own country, and executing anyone who questioned them. Resistance was futile, but trapping people in debt was against the Old Testament Scriptures so the snare was laid for Jesus. This is how the Bible, in Luke 20:20–26, records the incident.

Keeping a close watch on him, they sent spies, who pretended to be honest. They hoped to catch Jesus in something he said so that they might hand him over to the power and authority of the [Roman] governor. So the spies questioned him: 'Teacher, we know that you speak and teach what is right, and that you do not show partiality but teach the way of God in accordance with the truth. Is it right for us to pay taxes to Caesar or not?' He saw through their duplicity and said to them, 'Show me a denarius. Whose portrait and inscription are on it?' 'Caesar's,' they replied. He said to them, 'Then give to Caesar what is Caesar's, and to God what is God's.' They were unable to trap him in what he had said there in public. And astonished by his answer, they became silent.

'Is it right for us to pay taxes?' If Jesus had said 'No' he would have been arrested for sedition, and if he had said 'Yes' he would have lost his moral authority and would have been seen to be collaborating with the Romans, like the Jewish tax collectors he hung around with. Jesus did not squirm under the pressure or try to avoid the issue, but answered the question with a question to raise the conversation to a different level. Jesus asked whose image was on the coins and asserted unequivocally that the rightful owner should get what was rightfully theirs.

The coin had the image of Caesar stamped onto it, and therefore belonged to him. But everything ultimately belongs to God. The whole of creation, including the metal that is made into coins, belongs to God, and the whole of humanity, including Caesar himself, is made bearing God's image. Jesus' words challenged the religious and political leaders to look beyond Caesar, but at the same time clearly stated that Jesus was willing to allow the political order of his day, with all its corruption, to continue.

This reminds me of a Monty Python sketch called 'What have the Romans ever done for us?' After a typically amusing discourse, the sketch concludes that apart from better sanitation, medicine, education, irrigation, public health, roads, freshwater system, baths, public order . . . what did the Romans ever do for us?

Taxes are a way of sharing the cost of public services and Jesus is not opposed to them in principle. But Jesus does not give carte blanche to the Romans. Dorothy Day once put it like this: 'If we've given to God what is God's, there's not much left for Caesar.'[11] Jesus' followers are called to pay their taxes as good citizens so long as it does not contravene honouring God with the whole of their lives. However, if there is ever a choice between serving God or state, God always wins, as we are serve the state primarily out of worship to God. Dietrich Bonhoeffer and his friends made this distinction when they sought to take on the Nazi Party. They did not feel they were betraying their Christian calling to be good citizens, but holding to account a government that had betrayed its calling to serve the people. Jesus' words leave room for both civil obedience and civil disobedience.

In Jesus' day there were three main ways that Jewish believers were seeking to connect their faith and politics. What is interesting is that Jesus rejected all of them and gave us a new model to follow.

1 THE ZEALOTS combined faith and politics through terrorist acts of violence. Religiously motivated violence is nothing new, although the scale of its impact has vastly increased as radicalized religion is combined with the latest technology and a willingness to kill civilians in the name of ideology. Faith is not inherently dangerous, because atheism too has had its fair share of murderers and despots, but Jesus rejects this violent approach by forbidding his disciples to wield a sword, and commending the peacemakers. Nevertheless, Jesus is prepared to take former Zealots like Simon into his band of disciples.

2 THE ESSENES took the polar opposite view to the Zealots. Whereas the Zealots had a fight method of political engagement, the Essenes had a flight mentality, heading straight to the desert to set up an alternative society cut off from the corruption of the world. Jesus rejects this approach too, as he was commonly known as a friend of sinners, went to all the wrong parties, and spent time with all the social misfits and irreligious people the Essenes were trying to avoid.

3 THE PHARISEES had a compromise approach, offering support to the political system as long as the state left them alone to practice their religion, and upheld the religious hierarchy. The Pharisees would not challenge the power of Rome that had given them their status and position, but used it to their advantage when they wanted to get rid of troublemakers like Jesus. Jesus clearly rejects this approach in his outspoken critique of the hypocrisy of the Pharisees and their crime in twisting God's words to wield power over their flock.

So how does Jesus inspire us in political action? He inspires us to serve and respect the system, not use brute force and bullying like the Zealots. He inspires us to stay around and get involved, not hide away in a holy huddle like the Essenes. He inspires us to humility, courage and integrity, not cowardly compromise and manipulation like the Pharisees. Jesus had the power to impose a Christian way of life on the world – he is omnipotent almighty God. But instead, he comes as a servant, respecting human dignity enough to allow people the choice to follow him or not. Our call is to follow the King who came not to be served, but to serve. Our call is to give the government the respect it deserves out of reverence to the God we honour.

> **Voting, then, is not simply a right or a responsibility, but is part of our worship, act of loving service to God and our neighbour. Voting integrates the theological and the political. We vote, not simply for what is best for us, but what is best for others.**
>
> Votewise Now[30]

Are we who live in the more developed parts of the world to retreat into a cocoon of privilege while the storm rages elsewhere? Can we excuse ourselves with talk of compassion fatigue because we now see far more than we can do anything about? Are we to live in idleness because we can rationalize our rejection of the failures of idealism and do-goodery?

Os Guinness[42]

Section 4:

JUST
POLITICS
AND
GETTING
INVOLVED

THREE POLITICIANS CALL ON THE CHURCH

KRISH KANDIAH: How should Christians connect with political action? What are effective means of influence and involvement?

ANDY REED

Postcards and email postcards are the easiest way to connect and to show that you have something to say on a particular issue – but it is also the least effective method of influence as postcards are too easy. Postcards require very little effort, whereas composing your own letter requires more action so it makes me sit up and take notice.

GARY STREETER

I agree that postcards have a part to play – they portray a message and show the depth of feeling in your constituency about an issue, but it is just about the worst way a Christian can get involved in campaigning. It is much more effective to write your own individual letter setting out your own concerns and passions about an issue.

> **Stop doing wrong, learn to do right! Seek justice, encourage the oppressed.**
> **Defend the cause of the fatherless, plead the case of the widow.**
>
> Isaiah 1:17

One letter is worth about forty postcards. It probably takes three letters on the same subject to catch my attention and raise my interest, and if I get six or a dozen letters I know it's a crisis and I want to leap up and down and do something about it! If one person has taken the trouble to write a letter in their own words and in their own name, at least a hundred people probably feel the same, and it is therefore extremely effective.

ANDY REED

I got an email this week that caught my eye, along the lines of 'I am pretty appalled at the way asylum seekers are being treated in this country – what can I do?' This was, first of all, a brave viewpoint in a country in which asylum seekers are stigmatized by large parts of the media almost to the point of being subhuman. Secondly, this writer not only raised the issue to sound off to the MP and clear their conscience, but also expressed willingness to get involved. I would advise people: alongside writing letters, pray and get informed on the wider issues, join campaign groups like (in this case) the Refugee Council or Amnesty International, and work out if there is anything you can do. There may well be programmes running in your church or locality where you could volunteer, or you could start something like, for example, a drop-in coffee shop. Getting involved in big campaigns is relatively easy and, although it can make a difference, it is more important – although a lot harder – to 'love our neighbour' and put our faith into action on our own doorsteps.

STEVE WEBB

I agree that Christians should contact their local MP, and not only write to them about issues that they feel strongly about, but get to know what their MPs priorities are and what makes them tick. I think Christians should meet them and sound them out, especially on issues of justice and mercy, and ask them what they are going to do to make this a more just world. Voting is the next step in being involved in politics. When I go around knocking on doors, it is not the people who say, 'I vote for the other party' that disturb me, it is those who think that we are all the same, and there is no point in voting. Sometimes I notice that those who say they don't care about politics end up coming to visit me a few years later with a problem they need help with. Everyone should understand that the decisions that governments make at all levels have an impact on daily life. There are also vast amounts of money which are taken from one set of people and given to another set, sometimes this works well, sometimes it is not such a good idea, and we have influence over all these things in all tiers of government. The idea that this is of no interest to Christians or God is ridiculous, in my view. Every Christian needs to engage in politics by becoming informed and involved – at the very least, by exercising their power to vote.

> ## To be neutral in a situation of injustice is to have chosen sides already. It is to support the status quo. Desmond Tutu[25]

ANDY REED

Part of understanding why we should become engaged in politics is to see where power really lies. We as individual MPs are only part of the process, but my experience is that power lies elsewhere in the system. It was when I was chair of economic development on the borough council that I last made a decision and put it into action. Now I am little more than supreme lobbyist on behalf of my constituency and their views. The civil service, ministers and the number 10 policy unit have the power, and our tools of pressure are the media, Early Day Motions,[12] amendments, questions and private conversations. Policy can't actually move ahead without the civic society following, and vice versa. We need this twin-tracking as both work together in tandem. Sometimes, government is taking the lead and on other issues, the people are further ahead. It is increasingly possible to forge a greater interaction through technology, avoiding the triviality of an *X Factor* style democracy, but encouraging a greater sense of representation, co-operation and accountability.

GARY STREETER

I would encourage every Christian to join a political party. If I walked under a bus today, less than three hundred people would choose my successor, and that is for a safe Conservative seat. If the Christians in my constituency, who probably number several thousand, wanted to make a difference, they would have a significant say in selection and influence if they were members of a party. There are a number of single-issue groups that people can also join. Some are more respected than others, and the loudest ones are not necessarily the best. Unfortunately, some Christian campaign groups seem to be motivated by hate rather than love, and as a result their material is extreme, unpleasant and therefore rarely read, and ineffective in shaping politics. Other more thoughtful Christian lobby groups are very effective in working with government to come up with real solutions and ways forward.

Where I think we as Christians are missing a trick is by not getting together more to influence the local authority, police force, health service, education system and public life of the community. Not that we should be throwing the Bible around, or campaigning in the traditional sense, but I believe that if senior representatives of the churches acting together were to sit down with community leaders, not with an agenda but with an attitude of service, we would be able to exert very powerful pressure. Jubilee 2000 and Make Poverty History are very good national examples of churches joining together and politics aligning with public opinion. They have been extremely powerful as they put pressure on policymakers and national leaders to do things differently on global issues. I would like to see the church – which is the best-placed networked institution globally and historically – to grapple more with this in the next few years.

Finally, Christians can get involved in a party with a view to becoming an elected representative either at the local level, national level or European level. Three things I would ask anybody entering the political arena in this way: Firstly, do you feel this as a call on your life? Secondly, does your family support you in this? Thirdly, do you have strong Christians around you? The reality is that you are away from home a lot, and when the first flush of enthusiasm wanes and you go through good years and bad years, it is great to be able to call on likeminded people who understand what you are going through, and who will stand with you, pray with you, and cry with you. The political world is accessible and is made up of ordinary human beings trying by and large to do their best. So please try to understand them and pray for them, and if God touches you on the shoulder, understand that yes, you can do it too.

> This is what the LORD Almighty says: 'Administer true justice; show mercy and compassion to one another. Do not oppress the widow or the fatherless, the alien or the poor. In your hearts do not think evil of each other.'
>
> Zechariah 7:9,10

STEVE WEBB

I feel torn between the different roles that I have. I am the constituency representative, but I am not just a super-charged social worker. I am a legislator, and that has its challenges. I am a political reformer but I am also a party politician and I want my party to prosper. In a smaller party like mine, that means I have to not only work at home in my constituency and at parliament in London, but I also have to travel around the country visiting areas that do not have a Lib Dem seat, helping to campaign. That puts a lot of pressure on as I juggle the different roles, and I feel the frustration of wondering if I am doing any of the roles justice. Prayer support is vital for me and for MPs in similar positions.

ANDY REED

One of the ironies is that people often accuse their MPs of being out of touch, but the reality is that I hear views from the far left to the far right and everything in between on a regular basis, and I don't think I have ever felt more in touch! In my opinion, most people find themselves in a social circle of similarly-thinking friends and think the world agrees with them, when actually a lot of people disagree. For this reason, Christians should pray for wisdom for their MPs, who are considering the bigger picture and the wider perspective. In the Church of England there is a liturgy of prayer for our leaders, from the Queen and the government down to the local decision-makers. This is great, but it is even better when Christians give this some real thought, and even name those leaders.

GARY STREETER

Christians should definitely be praying for the family or home lives of their MPs, whether they are Christians or not, and that they would be open to influence from campaigns and issues in the constituency, not just take the party line by default. I would encourage all Christians to be proactive in prayer and be positive and supportive, and try to understand where the MPs are coming from, and be brave enough to go to see them from time to time, even if it is just to let them know they are being prayed for. It is difficult being a Christian in any job in the twenty-first century and being an MP or MEP is especially tough; most of us have to be away from home and family half the week, in the media spotlight, and every three to five years we have to stand before our people again and risk rejection and public humiliation.

A DAY IN THE LIFE OF . . .
STEVE WEBB MP

Breakfast meeting to discuss affordable housing – big issue in the towns and villages of my constituency

In office to check mountain of email messages and plan diary for coming weeks

Weekly meeting with senior Lib Dem MPs to consider forthcoming Westminster business

Coffee with national newspaper journalist to discuss possible story on pension campaign

Meet constituency tour group to answer questions

Attend lunchtime chapel service with MPs and staff from all parties

In House of Commons for oral questions to Department for Work and Pensions

90 minute committee debate on technical pension regulations

Evening in office catching up on emails and constituency correspondence

Final votes of day at 10 p.m. before phoning home and getting back to flat around 10.30 p.m.

Should Christians have anything to do with politics? Yes! If governments are to discharge their God-given duty of furthering God's purposes, they need the involvement of people who know what God's purposes are. We need politicians who are followers of Jesus in the House of Commons, in the House of Lords, in the Scottish and Welsh assemblies, in Stormont. In God's good providence, they are there. We need followers of Jesus in political parties, in local groups and party associations. In God's good providence, they are there. We need followers of Jesus in the media, in schools, in public service, in trade unions, in the civil service – anywhere where God's perspective can be contributed to the ongoing task of government. In God's providence they are there too. Ram Gidoomal[47]

DIGITAL DEMOCRACY

KRISH KANDIAH

Forget the family hush and huddle around the crackling wireless at 6 p.m. Forget the early morning trains full of commuters hiding behind their broadsheets. Staying informed in politics these days is so much easier. Now we can access politics through apps for our phone, widgets for our computers or bookmarks for our browsers.

Forget the placard at the gates of number 10. Forget the megaphone outside Television House, or the encouraging toots of a horn while driving past a local picket. Being a political agitator these days is even easier. Now to be an influencer all it takes is a few clicks of a mouse and we can be desktop demonstrators in a digital democracy.

We have never had so many opportunities to make sure that we know what our government is up to, and to make sure that what our government is up to has our say-so. Without even leaving the comfort of our desktop, we can be not only better informed, but more responsive, more connected and more influential than ever before. As politics meets social media, a whole new level of mass engagement and mobilization is born.

Take Barack Obama's campaign, for example. As canvassing went viral, the scale of his 2008 election operation was staggering. He had over 13 million people on his email list. He had 3 million online donors, 3 million mobile phone numbers for text updates, and 3 million friends on Facebook. He had 2 million web profiles and 80 million hits on official YouTube videos.

> **It seems inevitable that within a decade we will see a revolution coordinated by Twitter somewhere in the world.** Ian Hunt[45]

What Obama did was to democratize his campaign by empowering ordinary people to be his main supporters. In this way he proved that thousands of smaller donors could raise as much money as fewer rich elites who gave huge donations, and moreover that this method could mobilize thousands of advocates.

More and more politicians are recognizing that they can enlist supporters through online networks. But it is not only one-way traffic. Recently there have been three high profile cases that show how individuals through online networks can call politicians, press and companies to account and how, with relative ease, ordinary people can make a global difference.

When the Republican Party in the USA started to lambaste the National Health Service, citing horror stories of rationing, so many angry Britons responded by tweeting 'we love the NHS' that Twitter crashed. Gordon and Sarah Brown joined in the Twitter campaign alongside many thousands of ordinary people across the UK, adding weight to President Obama's campaign for reform in the US medical system.

Secondly, Twitter users in the UK forced a turnaround for the law firm Carter Ruck which managed to get a gagging order on *The Guardian* – preventing the newspaper from publishing information about questions raised by the MP Paul Farrelly regarding the behaviour of Trafigura. The oil company had suddenly announced that it would pay millions of pounds without any admission of liability

111

over allegations that it dumped toxic waste in the Ivory Coast in 2006, causing fifteen deaths and thousands of people to suffer from fume poisoning. Thanks to Twitter activists, the paper was allowed to publish details of the questions, which led to further action being taken to hold the oil company to account.

The third instance saw celebrity Twitter users Derren Brown and Stephen Fry at the forefront of a campaign to challenge what was deemed an aggressive, offensive and homophobic article written by Jan Moir of *The Daily Mail* on the events surrounding the death of Stephen Gately, a member of pop group Boyzone. The Press Complaints Commission received more complaints in a single weekend than in the previous five years, toting up over 21,000. The weight of the response was so strong that the PCC decided to explore the article, despite this being outside their normal criteria.

What can we learn from these high profile cases? Digital democracy is not something for 'Trekkies' and comic book futurologists. The future has arrived and without an appointment, a stamp or a newspaper, we can sit at home and play a strategic part in the public debate twenty-four hours a day, seven days a week. As *New York Times* journalist, David Carr observes: 'Yes, we have met Big Brother, the one who is always watching. And Big Brother is us.'[13]

Here are five simple and practical ways you can be a cyberpolitician:

1. TWITTER

Twitter involves sending messages of less than one hundred and forty characters, and is great for those of us who don't like writing lengthy letters or wading through vast tomes of political thought. Chances are your local MP is on Twitter and you can follow them as they give you succinct updates on their daily activities. Subscribe to http://tweetminster.co.uk/ to be kept up to date with the major debates going on in parliament. Join the debate by tweeting a Christian perspective on things that matter to God in the political realm.

2. FACEBOOK

Facebook is a social networking site, and you can update your profile with questions, comments and links to political debates that interest you. There are Facebook groups for people interested in expressing support for a variety of justice and political issues. I recently initiated a Facebook group to challenge the racist views being presented on BBC's *Question Time* by the BNP leader, claiming to be a Christian, called 'Nick Griffin does not speak for Christians'. Within ten days there were over three thousand five hundred members of the group. This was a simple and speedy way to unite Christians in challenging racism. Join Superbadger, which is an application designed by Tearfund to unite Facebook users in the fight against global poverty by badgering politicians or companies over issues of justice.

> **Thank you so much for all the supportive messages about our commitment to increase spending on international development. Over the last two months, my inbox has been inundated with hundreds of messages from you all. This is a great example of how social networks like Facebook can be used to campaign positively for the things people believe in, and I am really grateful to Tearfund for setting this up.**
> David Cameron[14]

3. COMMENT

Online newspapers are great – they are free, good for the environment and you can cut and paste great quotations for later personal use! Online newspapers are also great because most articles invite comment. This gives you an instant chance to respond to something that you have read, and gives feedback to the newspaper editors about what they are publishing. Make a comment if you consider the tone has been unfair, believe they are making a great point, or if you think there is an angle that has been missed.

> Truly we can't share the gospel with everyone, feed all the hungry, comfort all the afflicted or rescue all the oppressed, but all of us can, praise God, do something to advance these priorities of God. Gary Haughen[43]

4. THEY WORK FOR YOU

If, like me, you didn't even know the name of your local MP, let alone their views, values or voting records, then this is the website for you: www.theyworkforyou.com. You can sign up to receive a daily summary of what your MP has been saying on your behalf. You can click to send a letter (free of charge) to your MP. I have done this on a number of occasions; each time I have received a personal letter back within two weeks (www.writetothem.com).

5. FIX MY STREET

If local politics is more your concern, www.fixmystreet.com is a great site! You can use it to report a broken paving stone, fly tipping, littering, or out of control vegetation, simply by finding the area on a map and posting a message. I tried this site out by posting a concern about the street I live on, and received a response within hours.

Preventing the poorest of the poor from selling their products while we sing the virtues of the free market, that's not charity: That's a justice issue. Holding children to ransom for the debts of their grandparents, that's not charity: That's a justice issue. Withholding life-saving medicines out of deference to the Office of Patents, well that's not charity. To me, that's a justice issue.

Bono[39]

CASE STUDY: TEARFUND

It took 20 years for Muh Nasir to build his home but only seconds for the Indonesian earthquake to destroy it. As the first tremors shuddered the building, the father-of-five quickly gathered up his four-year-old daughter Ifah and took her into the garden. Panic-stricken, he realised another daughter, eight-year-old Mia, was missing and screamed for her to get out of the house. Just as she emerged into the safety of the outdoors, the property collapsed: 'Everything happened so fast and suddenly,' recalls Muh Nasir. Thankfully his wife and other children, who were elsewhere in the village of Cubadak Palak, were also safe. But ten others in the area didn't survive as some 970 homes were flattened. While Muh Nasir and his family escaped with their lives, the quality of those lives has been shattered. A tent is now the temporary home for Muh Nasir's family. As a low income labourer, getting a home in the first place took two decades of hard work and saving. He seems dazed and confused about how he will look after his family now: 'Earthquakes often happen in this area but this recent one is the hardest. We lost all our property which was so difficult to earn. I have to earn money over the next 20 years to build my house from the beginning and it will be hard for me especially in this economic crisis.'[15]

Consider how economics, environment and education are linked and impact people around the globe. What can and should the church be doing to help?

What should the government be doing to help?

Visit the Tearfund website (www.tearfund.org) for ways that you can get involved.

In 2004, 11,000 young people came to London to do an event called Soul in the City. They went out in their thousands across London to clean up graffiti, gardens, re-do people's homes. One group went round a tower block giving out window boxes they'd made full of flowers – at the end the tower block looked transformed! Many people came to know the love of Jesus that week and did so primarily through a practical display of God's care for those on the edge of society. At first the families of one estate were very suspicious of the 'Christians' arriving but they were totally overcome by the fact that the young people had paid to do this and the way in which they served. On the last day, to show their gratitude, the mums of the estate bought loads of ice cream, their little kids kept watch for the coaches of young people arriving, and when they saw them ran back to their mums shouting excitedly, 'The Christians are coming, the Christians are coming . . .!' The man who was heading the Metropolitan Police at the time said it had 'restored his faith in humanity'. The beauty of it was, this was all activity practically seeking to bring about the justice of God. When it happened people couldn't help but see the love of God.

Andy Croft, Associate Director of Soul Survivor

VISION FOR 2020

ANDY FLANNAGAN

So I'm praying, and I'm asking God to reveal what he wants to bring to pass in the realm of young people and politics. I feel an ever-so-kind kick up the backside as I realize that he already has! He has planted this stuff inside many young people the length and breadth of this country. As young people have encountered poverty and dysfunction during community action or international trips, their natural curiosity has led them to ask, 'Why are things they way they are?' They are not satisfied with the status quo. They are not satisfied with mere charity that allows us to feel we have done the right thing, without effecting long-term change. In the words of Martin Luther King, they realize many before them have been content to just be the Good Samaritan on life's roadside, but they want to improve the security of the Jericho Road so that no one else gets mugged. Having heard so often the adolescent cry of, 'It's not fair!' they are learning that injustice is often structural as well as personal. They are learning that until the global economic system is rewired according to principles of justice, rather than being ruled by the wealthy, any help we bring is quickly reversed. These facts are leading them to the natural conclusion that these things won't change while Christians are just shouting about them from the sidelines rather than getting on the pitch.

Politics is just people serving people. There shouldn't be anything more natural for a Christian. I stood as a candidate for a by-election in my local area last year; and as I knocked on people's doors and heard their stories, I realized that there was no one else knocking these people's doors. No one else was allowing them to feel connected to the bigger picture. And, to be honest, I wouldn't have been there if I wasn't looking for their vote. The imperfect yet brilliant thing that is democracy suddenly showed its worth. It is glue that holds society together.

I sit typing this not as naïve dreaming, but as genuine vision, because God has promised to redeem and restore all of creation, and politics is merely the way we organize ourselves in the midst of it. God's perfection *is* the future. It will happen. The only question is how soon, and you can be certain that we're the ones who will be the limiting factor, not God. We have the privilege of being partners with him in his project of 'making all things new' (see Rev. 21:5). Also bear in mind that I write this from the midst of a thoroughly depressed Labour HQ, in a week where nearly a million of my countrymen and women have voted for a party with a racist constitution, so my glasses are not rose-tinted.[16]

So here we go. In 2020 ...

Youth work in churches is missional. Young people are continually serving their communities. They understand that this is a vital part of the discipleship deal, rather than a fun summer extra. This engagement with their friends and community is breaking their hearts and forcing them to their knees. It is also highlighting where broken lives are a product of a broken society, so action is required not simply to mend individual lives but to mend the context in which they attempt to grow.

Young people are at the leading edge of an eschatological shift that has spread to the whole church. They see themselves as partners in God's restoration and redemption of all things. They see themselves as agents of the kingdom in the here and now. At youth gatherings they are commissioned to bring heaven on earth, rather than cajoled into buying an escape ticket for heaven. They are ruthless in their desire for justice and righteousness to burst forth in schools, supermarkets, youth clubs and the internet. They refuse the old 'either/or' of denominational or ecclesiological boundaries in favour of 'both/and'. They are just as comfortable lobbying a supermarket to stock fairly traded goods as they are praying for miraculous healing in the aisles of the same supermarket. They are just as comfortable speaking in the town hall as a local councillor as they are speaking in tongues in a brightly coloured prayer room.

Thus, local Conservative, Liberal Democrat and Labour branches are flooded with young Christians who always hold the kingdom above any political ideology, yet realize the need to find common cause, to engage and debate. They are building relationships that don't allow them to be pigeon-holed as 'crazy people'. They are listening and learning. They are serving and giving. They are blessing new friends, surprising them with gifts of fairly traded chocolate. They are invaluable because they turn up on time for meetings and they do what they say they will do before the next meeting. People can see evidence of 'the yeast working through the dough' (see Matt. 13:33) because there is a renewed integrity and enthusiasm about politics. They refuse to make politics about personality, or abuse people just because they are from 'the other side'. They campaign and make their case on the doorstep with a smile and a listening ear. This exposure to the reality of people's lives breaks their hearts and inspires much prayer as they walk around estates and suburbs.

It is as normal for a Christian young person to be pursuing a life in politics, as it is for them to aspire to be a worship leader. This calling is being affirmed and given space to grow. People are astounded that MPs are giving away so much of their money to good causes.

The days when they were claiming expenses for garden gnomes are long forgotten.

Worldwide attention is focused on Westminster because MPs are being miraculously healed in the corridors of power and legislation that 'Speak[s] up for those who cannot speak for themselves' (Prov. 31:8) is being enacted.

So how could this have come to pass?

Looking back, the twenty-somethings of the 'roaring twenties' realize that everything shifted when young people were encouraged to see *politics as mission*. When they put politics in the 'mission' part of their brains and hearts, they started to understand. In the same way that they would encourage, pray for, emulate, visit and support a 'missionary', they began to act like that towards those whose mission field was politics. It also changed when politics was presented as something exciting, countercultural and subversive, rather than the maintenance of the Establishment; just people serving people, rather than themselves.

> If there is light in the soul,
> There will be beauty in the person.
> If there is beauty in the person,
> There will be harmony in the house.
> If there is harmony in the house,
> There will be order in the nation.
> If there is order in the nation,
> There will be peace in the world.
> **Chinese Proverb**[35]

FACTFILE: TOP TEN THINGS TO PRAY FOR YOUR MPs

1 Pray, offer intercession and give thanks 'for kings and all those in authority, that we may live peaceful and quiet lives in all godliness and holiness. This is good, and pleases God our Saviour' (1 Tim. 2:1–3).

2 Pray that they would have the boldness to do what is right even when it is costly, both when they are and are not under the media spotlight.

3 Pray for a balance between their family life and their work life, a strong support network, and a clear sense of vocation.

4 Pray that they would work effectively, despite the pressures of juggling different roles.

5 Pray that they would see the fruit of their labour in their lifetime.

6 Pray for wisdom that they would consider the bigger picture and the wider perspective, not just take the party line by default.

7 Pray that they would be open to influence from campaigns and the wider constituency.

8 Pray for a sharp conscience so they can maintain their integrity and not tire, become complacent or hardened to the injustice in the world.

9 Pray that they would never become deaf to the voices of the poor, oppressed and marginalized.

10 Pray that they would live up to God's requirements – 'To act justly and to love mercy and to walk humbly' (Mic. 6:8).

SPEAKER'S CORNER: ENVIRONMENT

RUTH VALERIO

As I write, the annual season of party political conferences has just ended. Some of us may wonder how the words 'political conference' can occur in the same sentence as the word 'party', but for the members of the various political parties involved, they certainly seem to have enjoyed themselves.

At the start of this particular season, eight of the UK's biggest environmental groups issued a joint statement calling all the political parties to commit to ten green manifesto proposals and to sign up to what they called the Common Cause Declaration, which stated that climate change and restoring the natural environment should be accorded the highest priority during the next parliament.[17]

They're not alone in wanting to see this happen. Research carried out by *The Guardian* (and weighted to the profile of all adults) found that people (52 per cent) thought the environment should be the top priority, even more so than the economy (44 per cent).[18]

That's all well and good, but what about us as Christians? Should we be in that 52 per cent, or would we say that there are other issues that take precedence? Is this really something that we should be interested in, and should that be a factor in helping us decide who to vote for? I now vote Green in any election I'm involved with. In my area, that might be seen as a wasted vote and a silly thing

> '**But let justice roll on like a river, righteousness like a never-failing stream!**'
>
> Amos 5:24

to do, but for me it's an important statement of my beliefs. So why should the environment influence how we vote?

Firstly, because we are part of the environment. I actually really dislike the term 'environment': it implies that the rest of the world is like a stage that simply exists for us to act out our lives upon, and it creates an unhelpful distinction between humans and everything else. Actually, there is no 'environment', there is just the world that God has made and all the life that exists within it, including ourselves. From a purely selfish perspective, if the rest of the natural world suffers then ultimately we will too. For the sake of our own survival and wellbeing we have to sort out the mess that our world is in.

But it's not all about ourselves. Voting for a party that places a high priority on green matters is important because of the sad fact that when the natural world faces problems it's the poor who suffer most. As followers of Jesus, we worship a God who, at the heart of his agenda, has a concern for those who face poverty and injustice. We must do the same. Issues such as climate change aren't just about 'the environment'; they're also about the millions of people who are suffering today and will suffer in the future if we don't stop increasing levels of CO_2 going into the atmosphere.

And then, finally, this is important because, as Archbishop Rowan Williams said, 'the biblical picture presents us with a humanity that can never be itself without taking on the care and protection of the life of which it's a part'.[19] In other words, we have been created so that we might look after the rest of what God has made, and we are neither fully human nor fully Christian unless we remember that in all we do, including in how we vote.

The thing in all of this, though, is that the research in *The Guardian* goes on to say that, although 52 per cent think the environment should be top political priority, only 19 per cent say they would actually choose to pay more for a more expensive environmentally friendly product while shopping.[20] Let's not forget that what we do with our wallet is every bit as political as what we do with our ballot paper.

BIBLE: LAMB ON THE THRONE

KRISH KANDIAH

I couldn't resist. We were looking for a cheap secondhand family car – something practical and economical to ferry our toddlers around in. But when the salesman explained that under the bonnet of this reasonably priced car was a 2.5 litre turbo charged V6 engine – I was hooked. It was more power than I was ever going to need dropping my son off at nursery school. But, I reasoned, you can never have too much power ...

Whether it is horsepower, star power or political power, power is intoxicating. J.R.R. Tolkien's epic *Lord of the Rings* is a tale centring around the incredible power of the ring. But as the author shows how it brings misery and alters personalities, the book becomes a Christian commentary on the corrupting influence of power. Someone needs to carry the power but all too often, power falls into the hands, not of the wise, but of those who abuse their positions for sex, money, fame or revenge.

Throughout history, we have seen Christians take up positions of power, as well as stand back from accepting those positions. We have seen Christians at some times being disempowered, and at other times being overpowered. The Early Church could have felt overpowered as they faced fierce persecution under the Roman Empire. But God sent a vision to this struggling community, care of the exiled apostle John, to burn an image into their minds. That image was to help them withstand the abuse, hold on to hope, and re-engage with politics. It was an image that would have shocked first-century minds – a victim of the imperial might actually being the Victor in control of the universe; a slain lamb on the ultimate throne.

John, left to rot on the first-century island equivalent of Alcatraz, may well have thought that the throne in heaven was vacant, that God had abdicated and absconded, leaving the church to face suffering, and Caesar's throne as the ultimate authority. An empty throne in heaven would signify that chaos rules and that there is no ultimate accountability for humanity, no purpose to the universe, and would be an invitation for human beings to scramble for power for their own ends.

But God's vision in the book of Revelation shows an occupied throne. God is still there, despite the silence and the suffering and our frequent bewilderment at the injustice in the world. But the throne of God is occupied not by a man looking splendidly regal with crown and sword, but by a disfigured, slaughtered lamb. This is a powerful picture of Jesus and a perfect summary of his life and work. It reminds us of the cross of Jesus, where the Son of God and the rightful Ruler of the universe, voluntarily offered himself as a sacrifice.

It was no coincidence that Jesus was killed during the feast of Passover. This was one of the Jews' most precious festivals because it reminded them of a time when God had rescued them from abject slavery in Egypt. God had given them clear instructions to kill a lamb and paint its blood over the doors of their homes so

> # It is not good to be partial to the wicked or to deprive the innocent of justice.
> Proverbs 18:5

that the angel of death that was coming would know to 'pass over' the houses of those obedient to God. This marked the beginning of the exodus for the Jews as they were liberated from the abuse of the governmental power that held them captive, and they were set free to go and find their own land. When Jesus is described as the Lamb of God we are reminded of this event, the implication being that God's judgement is coming, that those who trust in the bloody sacrifice of Jesus on the cross will be spared, and that earthly powers will be revealed to be under God's ultimate control.

The picture of a Lamb on the throne speaks to our personal and political life. The One who sits on the throne does not do so in the safety of secluded grandeur, but as a victim himself. Jesus can sympathize with the marginalized and abused, those that have nothing and are victims of state bullying and exploitation. Jesus invites us to look to him for forgiveness and freedom and ultimate salvation.

In our political life, the picture of the Lamb on the throne demonstrates the example of power used well – the humble majesty of God himself is a model to rule not selfishly but sacrificially, whether we are those that occupy the seat of power or whether we simply have the responsibility of spending power, of using our influence through what we invest time in, who we will speak to, and how we will vote.

Lord Acton famously wrote in 1887, 'Power tends to corrupt and absolute power corrupts absolutely'[21] and world history has proved this time and again, with terrible consequences. But Christians do not believe this is the end of the story. There is hope. There is One who already has absolute power, who is not corrupted by power, but who conquers corruption through his humility. Jesus, the Lamb on the throne, put the needs of others before his own and demonstrated the transforming of power into service. We do not need to fear his power; although he is almighty beyond comparison, he is the servant King, the sacrificing conqueror.

Christians believe we have a model for engaging in politics because we follow the servant King who shows us how to use power humbly for others. But even in the midst of growing corruption and calamity and credit crunch, Christians also believe there is hope for politics because we know the story ends well. Economics will not have the final word: history does not belong to the bear or the bull. Neither does the future belong to the American eagle, the British lion or the Chinese dragon. It is the Lamb described in Revelation 5:6,8–10 that is the hope of the world.

> **Then I saw a Lamb, looking as if it had been slain, standing in the centre of the throne, encircled by the four living creatures and the elders. . . . Each one had a harp and they were holding golden bowls full of incense, which are the prayers of the saints. And they sang a new song: 'You are worthy to take the scroll and to open its seals, because you were slain, and with your blood you purchased men for God from every tribe and language and people and nation. You have made them to be a kingdom and priests to serve our God, and they will reign on the earth.'**

APPENDIX

FURTHER READING

Dave Bookless, *Planetwise: Dare to Care for God's World* (Leicester: IVP, 2008).

Shane Claibourne, *Jesus for President: Politics for Ordinary Radicals* (Grand Rapids, MI: Zondervan, 2008).

Paul Collier, *The Bottom Billion: Why the Poorest Countries are Failing and What Can Be Done About It* (Oxford: OUP, 2008).

Joel Edwards, *An Agenda for Change: A Global Call for Spiritual and Social Transformation* (Grand Rapids, MI: Zondervan, 2008).

Ram Gidoomal and David Porter, *How Would Jesus Vote?* (Oxford: Monarch Books, 2001).

Donald Hay, *Economics Today: A Christian Critique* (Vancouver: Regent College, 2001).

Gary Haughen, *Good News about Injustice: A Witness of Courage in a Hurting World* (Leicester: IVP, 1999).

Marijke Hoek and Justin Thacker: *Micah's Challenge: The Church's Responsibility to the Global Poor* (Carlisle: Paternoster, 2008).

Rose Lynas, ed., *Votewise Now! Helping Christians engage with the issues* (London: SPCK, 2009).

Andy Reed, *Faith and Politics: Engage or Escape* (Ilkeston: Headway Publications, 2004).

Jeffrey Sachs, *The End of Poverty: How We Can Make It Happen in Our Lifetime* (London: Penguin, 2005).

Ronald J. Sider, *The Scandal of Evangelical Politics: Why are Christians Missing the Chance to Really Change the World* (Grand Rapids, MI: Baker Books, 2008).

Nick Spencer and Jonathan Chaplin, *God and Government* (London: SPCK, 2009).

Alan Storkey, *Jesus and Politics: Confronting the Powers* (Grand Rapids, MI: Revell, 2005).

Ruth Valerio, *L is for Lifestyle: Christian Living That Doesn't Cost the Earth* (Leicester: IVP, 2008).

Jim Wallis, *God's Politics: Why the American Right Gets it Wrong and the Left Doesn't Get it* (Oxford: Lion Hudson, 2006).

Jim Wallis, *Seven Ways to Change the World: Reviving Faith and Politics* (Oxford: Lion Hudson, 2008).

Richard Wilkinson and Kate Pickett: *The Spirit Level: Why More Equal Societies Almost Always Do Better* (London: Allen Lane, 2009).

John Howard Yoder: *The Politics of Jesus* (Grand Rapids, MI: Eerdmans, 1996).

LIST OF CONTRIBUTORS

MPs

Andy Reed is the Labour and Co-operative MP for Loughborough. He is one of twenty-nine Labour and Co-op Party MPs in the House of Commons and actively promotes the principles of co-operation, both locally and nationally, particularly in the field of economic development, credit unions and the social economy. He also has a passion for sport, chairing regional and national sports boards as well as belonging to numerous parliamentary sports teams. He advises the Board of Christian Solidarity Worldwide, speaks at Spring Harvest, and sits on the council of the Evangelical Alliance.

Gary Streeter is the Conservative MP for Devon South West (which includes the Plymouth suburbs of Plympton and Plymstock). He has worked in the Whip's office, in the Lord Chancellor's Department, as Shadow Secretary of State for International Development, as Vice Chairman of the Conservative Party, on the Conservative Human Rights Commission, and as a member of the Home Affairs Select Committee. His latest appointment is to the Chairman's Panel, chairing the weekly committees and debates that take place in the House of Commons.

Steve Webb is the Member of Parliament for Northavon and the Liberal Democrat Shadow Secretary of State for Work and Pensions. He has worked as Shadow Secretary of State for the Environment, Energy, Food and Rural Affairs, and shadowed the new Department for Energy and Climate Change when it was created in October 2008. He is also part of a small group of advisers who meet regularly with party leader Nick Clegg to consider the best policy response to the recession.

SERIES EDITOR

Krish Kandiah is Executive Director for Evangelical Alliance: Churches in Mission. He is a speaker, lecturer, writer, foster carer, church leader and author of a number of books to help Christians connect the gospel with their day-to-day lives.

OTHER CONTRIBUTORS

Lyndon Bowring is the Executive Chairman of CARE. CARE is a Christian charity providing resources and helping to bring Christian insight and experience to matters of public policy and practical caring initiatives. CARE is represented in the UK Parliaments and Assemblies, as well as at the EU and the UN.

Gordon Brown is the Prime Minister of the United Kingdom and Leader of the Labour Party, having previously served as Chancellor of the Exchequer in the Labour government from 1997 to 2007.

David Cameron is the British Member of Parliament for Witney, leader of the Conservative Party and Leader of the Opposition.

Nick Clegg is the British Member of Parliament for Sheffield Hallam and leader of the Liberal Democrat Party.

Ben Cooley is the founder and CEO of Hope for Justice, which exists to inspire a new generation of Christians known for living out the gospel through justice and righteousness.

Andy Croft is Associate Director of Soul Survivor. A theology graduate from Cambridge University, Andy now runs events around the world which seek to equip young people to worship God and live missionally.

Joel Edwards is the International Director of Micah Challenge, a global campaign to mobilize Christians against poverty, and to influence leaders of rich and poor nations to fulfil their promise to achieve the Millennium Development Goals. He is also a Commissioner for the Equality and Human Rights Commission in the UK.

Andy Flannagan is the Director of the Christian Socialist Movement. He is also an Irish singer songwriter with a heart for global justice, who has sung for MPs and Gordon Brown. Many of his songs are used by NGOs such as Tearfund, Christian Aid, Stop the Traffik, Stop Climate Chaos and Make Poverty History, as well as in the national media.

Andy Frost is a church planter, a surfer, a dreamer, a schemer and Director of Share Jesus International, which is a Christian charity passionate about innovating and creatively engaging with the world, and dedicated to mission, mobilizing the church to further action and demonstrating God's heart for justice.

Charis Gibson is the Senior Press Officer for the Evangelical Alliance. She moved to Public Relations after six years as a reporter on regional newspapers, where she specialized in crime reporting and campaigns, and also covered two general elections.

Ram Gidoomal is a businessman, social entrepreneur and author. He was a former independent candidate for London Mayor and Greater London Assembly, and is a tireless worker for charity and raising social concern over the poor.

Donald Hay is an economist, who has researched and written on Christian ethics and economic analysis. Formerly he was Head of the Division of Social Sciences at Oxford University. Currently he is the leader of the Developing a Christian Mind programme in Oxford, which seeks to enable Christian graduate students, researchers and academic staff in the universities to integrate their faith with research and scholarship.

Jon Kuhrt is the Director of Community Mission at Livability (formerly the Shaftesbury Society), an organization supporting urban mission and resourcing the church to combat poverty, isolation and despair. He is also a member of the Christian Socialist Movement and Labour Party, and writes articles about Christian social and political responsibility.

Dave Landrum is the Senior Parliamentary Officer for the Bible Society. Based in parliament he works on raising the profile and influence of the Bible in political culture, supporting the Christian community in Westminster, and developing more effective and extensive Christian political engagement.

Patsy McKie is the Chair of Mothers Against Violence, an organization that promotes the eradication of violence, and provides relief for the victims of the effects of gun and knife crime within the community.

Lauri Moyle is a Fellow of the Institute for Faith and Culture and works for CARE as a Public Affairs Officer. He volunteers with a political party in his local constituency, working with councillors and parliamentary candidates.

Alan Storkey is a Christian political theorist, economist, writer and lecturer and author of a number of books on Christian faith, society and politics, most recently *Jesus and Politics: Confronting the Powers*. He is also the former Chairman of the Movement for Christian Democracy.

Ruth Valerio runs A Rocha's Living Lightly project and is the author *L is for Lifestyle: Christian Living That Doesn't Cost the Earth*. She is doing doctoral studies at Kings College London, and spends much of her time speaking and writing on issues of justice and the environment.

Danny Webster is the Parliamentary Officer for the Evangelical Alliance working closely with lawmakers and public theologians to respond to new policies and political challenges. He also works with churches in the vital role they can play to shape the political process through campaigns and longer term strategic engagement.

NOTES

[1] David Kinnaman, *UnChristian: What a New Generation Really Thinks About Christianity . . . And Why It Matters* (Grand Rapids, MI: Baker Books, 2007).

[2] Roy Hattersley, *The Guardian*, Monday 12 September 2005.

[3] Permission granted to quote.

[4] Adapted from the Collins English Dictionary.

[5] See www.un.org/millennium/declaration/ares552e.htm, article 11.

[6] Chris Wright, *The Mission of God: Unlocking the Bible's Grand Narrative* (Leicester: IVP, 2006).

[7] Geoff Mulgan, *Good and Bad Power* (London: Penguin, 2007), p.3.

[8] Desmond and Naomi Tutu, *The Words of Desmond Tutu* (New York: Newmarket Press, 2008), p.30.

[9] Chuck Colson is Founder of Prison Fellowship Ministries and author of the book *Born Again* (New Jersey: Chosen Books, 1976). He was embroiled in the Watergate Scandal when he was Special Counsel for President Richard Nixon.

[10] See www.fulcrum-anglican.org.uk/page.cfm?ID=94.

[11] Dorothy Day quoted in Charles Colson, Gregory Boyd and Shane Claiborne, 'Three Leaders, Three Generations, debate whether political involvement is a duty or distraction for the church', in *Leadership Journal*, 19 September 2008.

[12] Early Day Motions are formal motions submitted for debate in parliament. They are rarely debated, but are good for raising media coverage and public attention.

[13] http://www.nytimes.com/2008/11/10/business/media/10carr.html (accessed 17.11.09).

[14] In response to a 'badger' thanking him for prioritizing overseas aid (permission to quote granted).

[15] Reproduced from www.tearfund.org www.tearfund.org Copyright © Tearfund UK 2009.

[16] European Elections June 2009.

[17] *Common Cause: The Green Standard Manifesto on Climate Change and the Natural Environment*, authored by CPRE, Friends of the Earth, Green Alliance, Greenpeace, RSPB, The Wildlife Trusts, Woodland Trust and WWF (18.9.09), http://www.green-alliance.org.uk/grea_p.aspx?id=4412.

[18] www.guardian.co.uk/environment/2008/jul/02/climatechange.ethicalliving (accessed 14.10.09).

[19] Archbishop Rowan Williams, 'The Climate Crisis: a Christian Response', lecture at Southwark Cathedral (13.10.09).

[20] See above.

[21] www.phrases.org.uk/meanings/288200.html.

[22] http://www.parliament.uk/about/how/business/prayers.cfm.

[23] www.publications.parliament.uk/pa/ld/ldcomp/ldctso58.htm.

[24] Shane Claiborne, *Jesus for President: Politics for Ordinary Radicals* (Grand Rapids, MI: Zondervan, 2008).

[25] Desmond and Naomi Tutu, *The Words of Desmond Tutu* (New York: Newmarket Press, 2008), p.30.

[26] Quoted in Henlee Hulix Barnette, *A Pilgrimage of Faith: My Story* (Macon, GA: Mercer University Press), p.166.

[27] Quoted in Jonathon Green, *A Cynic's Lexicon: A Dictionary of Amoral Advice* (London: Routledge, 1984), p.164. Originally in The New York Times (Wednesday 12 June 1968) p.46.

[28] Quoted in Daniel C. Cohn-Sherbok and David McLellan, *Religion in Public Life* (New York: Palgrave MacMillan, 1992) p.86.

[29] Barack Obama, *Dreams of my Fathers* (Edinburgh: Canongate Books, 2008), p.xi.

[30] Rose Lynas, ed., *Votewise Now! Helping Christians engage with the issues* (London: SPCK, 2009), p.5.

[31] Speech to Faithworks 22 March 2005 http://politics.guardian.co.uk/speeches/story/0,,1443467.00.html quoted in Graham Cray, *Disciples and Citizens* (Leicester: IVP, 2007), p.182.

[32] Andy Reed, *Faith and Politics: Engage or Escape* (Ilkeston: Headway Publications, 2004), p.5.

[33] Speech marking the Voting Rights Act, Washington DC, 6 August 1965.

[34] Letter written from jail, 16 April 1963. Martin Luther King Jr, *The Autobiography of Martin Luther King Jr* (New York: Warner Books, 2001), p.343.

[35] Tim Porter-O'Grady, *Quantum Leadership: A Textbook of New Leadership* (Sudbury, MA: Jones and Bartlett Publishers, Inc., 2005), p.324.

[36] In ed. Leopold Labedz, *Solzhenitsyn: A Documentary Record* (London: Penguin, 1974), p.151.

[37] National Prayer Breakfast Speech quote, www.usatoday.com/news/washington/2006-02-02-bono-transcript_x.htm.

[38] National Prayer Breakfast Speech quote, as above.

[39] National Prayer Breakfast Speech quote, as above.

[40] Quoted by Winston Churchill (Sinews Speech). Martin Gilbert, *Churchill, Great Lives Observed* (New Jersey: Prentice-Hall, 1967), p.49.

[41] Quoted in Os Guinness, *Unspeakable* (London: HarperCollins, 2005), p.1.

[42] Quoted in Os Guinness, *Unspeakable* (London: HarperCollins, 2005), p.236.

[43] Gary Haughen, *Good News About Injustice* (Leicester: IVP, 1999), p.176.

[44] Gary Haughen, *Good News About Injustice* (Leicester, IVP, 1999), p.68.

[45] Ian Hunt: www.politics.co.uk/sketch/culture-media-and-sport/comment-twitter-is-changing-politics-forever-$1335209.htm.

[46] Quoted in the foreword to ed. M. Hoek and J. Thacker, *Micah's Challenge: The Church's Responsibility to the Global Poor* (Milton Keynes: Paternoster, 2008).

[47] Ram Gidoomal with David Porter, *How Would Jesus Vote?* (Oxford: Monarch Books, 2001), p.154.

[48] Adapted version bt Andy Flannagan of his song 'Arms', © Daybreak Music Ltd. Admin by Memralife. Used by permission.